The Anglican Cycle of Prayer

2003

Updated information for the
Anglican Cycle of Prayer
is available in *Anglican World*

Partnership House
157 Waterloo Road
London SE1 8UT
England

or on the web at
www.forwardmovement.org
www.anglicancommunion.org

Published for the Anglican Consultative Council

412 Sycamore Street, Cincinnati, Ohio 45202, USA

Church House Publishing, Church House,
Great Smith Street, London SW1P 3NZ, England

Table of Contents

ARCHBISHOP
OF CANTERBURY

Dear Friends

Prayer has been the engine of my ministry as Archbishop of Canterbury. It has helped both my wife, Eileen, and myself to hold fast to the ministry that God had given us in the Anglican Communion. Bishops, clergy and lay people from all around the Communion often tell me that week by week or on special days the work of the Archbishop of Canterbury was being remembered in prayer. Such knowledge has made a real difference in how I have carried out my ministry over the years. I want to thank my brothers and sisters throughout the Communion for their prayers and the time they take to pray for one another. Through this means we commit ourselves to becoming more and more a true Communion of Churches worldwide.

I will remember the many faces, the smiles, the sounds, and sights of the Provinces that I have visited, including my own Church of England. Such memories will aid my reliance on the Anglican Cycle of Prayer in asking God's blessing on the Anglican Episcopal family of Churches in the years ahead.

I am grateful to Forward Movement Publications and the Anglican Communion Office for publishing such a fine instrument to help us focus our thoughts, concerns and heart-felt prayers

Your brother in Christ

+ George Cantuar

Lambeth Palace, London SE1 7JU

Anglican Cycle of Prayer—2003

The Anglican Communion is a diverse fellowship spanning the globe. As members of the Communion we are called to be "members one of another," to be brothers and sisters in Christ. Through prayer our unity in Christ can be most fully experienced. Prayer is the activity of the Spirit who unites us with God, ourselves and our neighbors. It forms within us the very longing of Christ, "that all may be one," and catches us up into God's own project of breaking down walls of division and making us, in all our singularity and uniqueness, into one new humanity in Christ (Ephesians 2:15).

The Anglican Cycle of Prayer is invaluable in that it brings us into each other's daily lives, lifting each of us out of our own reality and context into the triumphs and struggles of our neighbors. If we take seriously the notion that we through baptism are limbs of Christ's risen body then it is through us–our words, our relationships, our deeds, our very being–that Christ continues to be present in the world and to give himself away in a continual outpouring of reconciling love. Our prayers for one another remind us continually of the Holy Spirit's gift of unity and the responsibility to one another which that gift entails.

Through our prayers may we come to a better understanding of one another in Christ and embrace fully the gift of our Communion. May we together share Christ's love with all of God's people throughout our broken world, which yearns for healing and reconciliation.

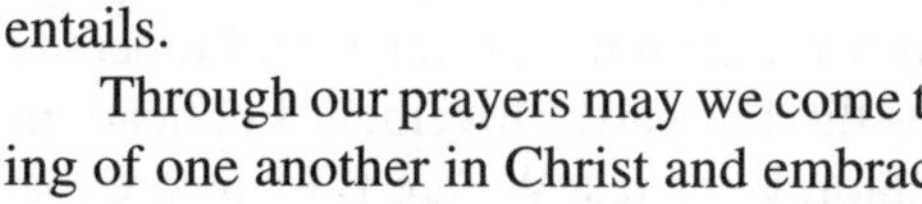

The Most Rev. Frank T. Griswold
Presiding Bishop and Primate
The Episcopal Church, USA

PREFACE

Pray without ceasing...

— I Thessalonians 5.xvii

Beloved friends in Christ:

The 2003 edition of *The Anglican Cycle of Prayer* represents a departure in format and content from previous editions. We are returning to an annual edition, having learned that a two-year cycle was impossible to update, especially with episcopal appointments and new dioceses. These realities come with the fact that the churches are growing and change is ever with us.

We hope that, when praying for a diocese, our clergy and people around the world will pray, "For the Bishops, clergy and laity of the Diocese of ________."

With the recent announcement of our new Archbishop of Canterbury, the Most Rev'd. Rowan Douglas Williams, we can assure him and our own primates of our prayers for them on a regular basis.

With the advent of internet accessibility and websites of nearly all of the Churches in our Communion, we encourage you to check those sites for current episcopal and diocesan information, as well as the Forward Movement Publications and Anglican Communion websites. We are fully aware that not all have the same access to current technology and thus want to offer the best we can for all of our fellow Anglicans.

This edition includes two sections for the user, to assist in their prayer life, in public and in private. The first is the 52-week cycle for 2003 that highlights the National Church or Province for the coming week. It includes the history and contact information about the Province.

Section two is a 365-day prayer cycle that includes dioceses by name and special intentions for Holy Days, Feasts and Fasts. Some of the dates include as many as 15 dioceses; some only one; and some special intentions. During communal liturgies, we suggest clergy and officiants determine which intentions best suit their worshipping community's needs, and adapt from the list or write their own for the day.

The Anglican Cycle of Prayer is not writ in stone; it is simply a guide to assist us in remembering one another in prayer. Local adaptation is important and essential.

As we look to the future, we believe we will witness ever-greater use of the internet and CD-ROM media as a means of distributing mutual concerns and intentions throughout the Communion. Your comments, suggestions and prayers are asked as we seek to improve this most important aspect of our life as a Communion, our Common Prayer.

We join in bidding each of you God's blessing and every mercy, peace in our world and in all our hearts.

The Rev. George C. Allen II
Forward Movement Publications
Cincinnati, Ohio

Canon James M. Rosenthal II
Anglican Communion
Communications Officer
London

The hymn beloved by Anglicans all over the world tells us "The voice of prayer is never silent".

Indeed the daily rhythm of worship that supports the cathedrals, churches, chapels, convents, monasteries and schools of the Anglican Communion is a constant reminder of our inter dependence in the Body of Christ.

It is my particular joy to ask the prayers of our family for our newly announced 104th Archbishop of Canterbury, the Most Rev'd. Rowan Williams, Archbishop of Wales. The office of the Archbishop of Canterbury is one that has many demands placed upon it and I would hope that we will encourage our new spiritual leader in the Anglican Communion remembering him and his family at the altars of all our sacred institutions on a regular basis. As our journey to unity continues, it is one that has in its heart great tradition of Anglican worship, liturgy and music and yet is open to the spirit in making all things new and fresh for the glory of God and edification of God's people.

I commend this new *Anglican Cycle of Prayer* to you for your fervent use in the hope that we can be confident we are remembering each other in the presence of God.

The Rev'd. Canon John L. Peterson
Secretary General
The Anglican Consultative Council

Suggestions on How to Use the *Anglican Cycle of Prayer*

Public worship

On Sundays, include the province (or other intention) in your general intercessions: Today we pray for ____*(place)*____ or ____*(intention)*____.

Some churches remember *all* the specific intentions for the week.

Include the intentions from the *Anglican Cycle of Prayer* in your list of printed parish intercessions.

In weekday services that include general intercessions, include the diocese (or other intention).

At special diocesan or provincial gatherings, include that day's *Anglican Cycle of Prayer* intention as a reminder of your link to the Anglican Communion.

Private prayer (personal prayers)

Include that day's intention in your daily prayers.

Study

Use the *Anglican Cycle of Prayer* as a basis for an adult study group.

Use as a reference book.

Anglican Cycle of Prayer

A Weekly Guide for the Year of Our Lord 2003

FROM JANUARY 1, 2003

GIVE THANKS for the extra-provincial Diocese of Bermuda.

WEEK OF JANUARY 5, 2003 *Christmas 2*

GIVE THANKS for the Church of Myanmar (formerly Burma).

Country: Myanmar
Dioceses: 6 (Hpa-an; Mandalay; Mytikyina; Sittwe; Toungoo; Yangon)
Provincial mailing address:
Bishopscourt
140 Pyidaungsu Yeiktha Road
Dagon PO (11191)
Yangoon, Myanmar

WEEK OF JANUARY 12, 2003 *1 Epiphany — Baptism of Our Lord*

GIVE THANKS for the Anglican Church of Australia.

The Province was founded in 1876.
Country: Australia
Dioceses: 23 (Adelaide; Armidale; Ballarat; Bathurst; Bendigo; Brisbane; Bunbury; Canberra and Goulburn; Gippsland; Grafton; Melbourne; Newcastle; North Queensland; North West Australia; Northern Territory; Perth; Riverina; Rockhampton; Sydney; Tasmania; The Murray; Wangaratta; Willochra)
Geographical area: 2,967,905 square miles

Population: 17,752,829
Number of Anglicans: 3,903,324
Number of Christians: 12,582,764
Other faiths: 616,428
Number of parishes: 3,313
Number of clergy: 2,036
Provincial mailing address:

Anglican General Synod Office
P.O. Box Q190
Queen Victoria Post Office
Sydney, New South Wales 2000
Australia

WEEK OF JANUARY 19, 2003 *2 Epiphany*

Week of Prayer for Christian Unity.

WEEK OF JANUARY 26, 2003 *3 Epiphany*

The Archbishop of Canterbury

WEEK OF FEBRUARY 2, 2003 *The Presentation*

GIVE THANKS for the Province of the Indian Ocean (Provansa Eklesiastikan'ny Oseana Indiana) (Province Ecclesiastique De L'Ocean Indien).

Initially this region comprised two dioceses: Madagascar and Mauritius, which were divided respectively into three and two in 1969, thus permitting the creation of the Province in 1973 with its five dioceses. As the Province is made up of three independent states with different histories and cultures, unity in diversity is lived by experience, and proves to be a source of strength and richness. Since 1996 Antsiranana (ex-Diego-Suarez) was divided into two and gave birth to the new small, but fast growing, diocese of Mahajanga. French is the official language of the Province. However, Seychelles and Mauritius are trilingual (with English and Creol) and Madagascar mainly bilingual (Malagasy and French). To date four Archbishops successively led the Province.

Countries: Madagascar, Mauritius, Seychelles
Dioceses: 7 (Antananarivo; Antsiranana; Fianarantsoa; Mahajanga; Mauritius; Seychelles; Toamasina)
Geographical area: 230,223
Population: 14,470,000
Number of Anglicans: 120,000
Number of Christians: 6,928,000
Other faiths: Muslim, Hindus
Number of parishes: 86
Number of clergy: 114
Provincial mailing address:
Evêché Anglican - Lot VK57 ter
Ambohimanoro
101 Antananariovo, Madagascar

WEEK OF FEBRUARY 9, 2003 *5 Epiphany*

GIVE THANKS for the Church of the Province of Burundi.

The first missionaries to reach Burundi, Roman Catholic White Fathers, arrived in 1898 from Tanganyika. British Anglican missionaries arrived in 1935, sent by Rwanda Mission, a branch of the Church Missionary Society. Accompanied by Rwandans and Ugandans from the East

Africa Revival, they focused on evangelism, education and medical work. The church grew as catechists, on foot, established tiny congregations across the country. The first Burundian priests were ordained in 1954. One of them, Yohana Nkunzumwami, became the first Burundian Bishop in 1965. In 1985, the president of Burundi expelled almost all expatriate missionaries, imprisoned many church leaders and repossessed much church property. The present government has changed this policy. The church of Burundi was part of the Francophone province of Burundi, Rwanda and Zaire until 1992 when it became an independent Province.

Three peoples—Tutsi, Hutu and Twa (Pygmy)—make up the populace of this small nation, about the size of Massachusetts. They share one language, one culture and one territory. But germs of social injustice existed within the Burundi traditional society, affecting all of the ethnic groups.

The current civil war has meant 600,000 people displaced internally and 300,000 forced to flee as refugees to other countries. The need for assistance— food, shelter, clothing—is overwhelming. So is the need for the church's ministry of preaching, teaching and caring.

The Episcopal Church of the Province of Burundi is a minority presence in this predominantly Roman Catholic nation. Its catechists and priests are ministering in difficult and dangerous situations. Some priests and pastors have been killed. Some churches have had to close in areas where the fighting is intense.

Development offices in the Province's five dioceses oversee efforts in agriculture, animal husbandry health and improving water supply. Income-generating projects such as raising chickens and cereal mills help people maintain hope even as neighboring countries enforce an economic blockade that makes life ever more difficult. Community development—education, social work, poverty eradication—is a major focus. Through income generating projects the church hopes to contribute to a sustainable development. Hygiene and primary health care are also needed, especially among the displaced and in the regroupment camps, where there are many epidemic diseases, such as the outbreak of typhus in the Spring of 1997. Mortality rates could not be determined but some believe that as many as 20 percent of those infected died.

The poverty is visible in the church. A priest's salary may be as little as $10 per month. Yet with all its struggles the church is growing.

Country: The Republic of Burundi

Dioceses: 5 (Bujumbura; Buye; Gitega; Makamba; Matana)

Geographical area: 10,740 square miles

Population: 5,943,057

Number of Anglicans: 300,000

Number of Christians: 85 percent (Roman Catholics, 65 percent; Protestants, 20 percent)

Other faiths: Traditional beliefs, 10 percent; Muslims, 3 percent

Number of parishes: 150

Number of clergy: 170 Priests

Provincial mailing address:

B. P. 2098
Bujumbura, Burundi

WEEK OF FEBRUARY 16, 2003 *6 Epiphany*

GIVE THANKS for the Province of Hong Kong Sheng Kung Hui.

Countries: Peoples Republic of China, Macao
Dioceses: 3 (Eastern Kowloon; Hong Kong Island; Western Kowloon)
Provincial mailing address:
Province of Hong Kong
Bishop's House
1 Lower Albert Road
Hong Kong, Peoples Republic of China

WEEK OF FEBRUARY 23, 2003 *7 Epiphany*

GIVE THANKS for the Church of the Province of Central Africa.

The first missionaries to what is now Zimbabwe arrived in 1560 when the Roman Catholic bishop of Mozambique sent a group of Jesuits. Those missions ended in failure. The emperor turned against the newcomers. Later Christian missions, at the end of the 19th century, fared better when African evangelists came to preach and lay the ground work. The diocese of Central Africa was formed in 1861 under the leadership of Bishop Charles F. Mackenzie. The Anglican Church expanded into parts of the region from the coast of South Africa with help from the Society for the Propagation of the Gospel. British colonial administrations gave lands to such mission organizations for schools, hospitals, mission reserves. The Province of Central Africa was founded in 1955 with the union of the Diocese of Northern Rhodesia, Nyasaland,

Mashonaland, and Matabeleland.

The Province has had to face problems forced in from outside its borders—refugees from Rwanda, Burundi and Zaire. In Zambia, with "very slender resources," the church helped form Zairian, Burundese and Rwandese refugee associations, working with their leaders to see that aid goes where it is most needed.

Traditional religion and traditional practices continue throughout the Province of Central Africa and many Christians practice both religions, melding the two observances. Independent, African initiated, they are estimated to be 10,000 or more across the continent and are another phenomenon to be dealt with.

While running the risk of syncretism the independent churches demonstrate a pride that cannot be denied. As the archbishop says, "A church in Africa that does not understand community—and it is a direct challenge to Western emphasis of individual salvation—will always be in trouble. People know, from their culture, that they belong to the community of the unborn, the living and the death. A church that takes no notice of that is in trouble."

Countries: Botswana, Malawi, Zambia, Zimbabwe

Dioceses: 12 (Botswana; Central Zambia; Central Zimbabwe (The Lundi); Eastern Zambia; Harare; Lake Malawi; Lusaka; Manicaland; Matabeleland; Northern Zambia; Northern Malawi; Southern Malawi)

Geographical area: 718,940 square miles

Population: 31,786,482

Number of Anglicans: 600,000 (figure from early 1990s)

Number of Christians: 47 percent

Other faiths: Traditional beliefs, 20 percent; Muslim, 15 percent; Syncretic beliefs, 15 percent
Number of parishes: 250 parishes, with 10-30 congregations each
Number of clergy: 400 (figure from early 1990s)
Provincial mailing address:
P.O. Box 769
Gaborone, Botswana

WEEK OF MARCH 2, 2003 *Last Epiphany*

GIVE THANKS for the Anglican Church in Mexico.

Country: Mexico
Dioceses: 5 (Cuernavaca; Mexico; Northern Mexico; Southeastern Mexico; Western Mexico)
Number of parishes: 12
Number of congregations 121
Provincial mailing address:
Fco. Javier Gamboa #255
Col. Sector Juarez
44100 Guadalajara, Jal
Mexico

WEEK OF MARCH 9, 2003 *Lent 1*

GIVE THANKS for the Province of Episcopal Church of Rwanda (PEER) (Eglise Episcopale au Rwanda) (Provinsi y'Itorero ry'Ubwepikopi mu Rwanda).

The Province of the Episcopal Church of Rwanda came into being in 1992. Previously it had been a part of the enormous Anglican Province of Zaire, Rwanda and Burundi.

Country: Rwanda
Dioceses: 9 (Butare; Byumba; Cyangugu; Gahini; Kibungo; Kigali; Kigeme; Shyira; Shyogwe)
Geographical area: 26,338 square kilometers
Population: 7,000,000
Number of Anglicans: 1,019,763
Number of Christians: 5,600,000
Other faiths: 380,237
Number of parishes: 197
Number of clergy: 297
Provincial mailing address:

The Province of Episcopal Church of Rwanda (PEER)
B.P. 2487
Kigali, Rwanda
Africa

WEEK OF MARCH 16, 2003 *Lent 2*

GIVE THANKS for the Church of Ireland.

Countries: The Republic of Ireland and Northern Ireland
Dioceses: 12 (*Armagh:* Armagh; Clogher; Connor; Derry and Raphoe; Down and Dromore; Kilmore, Elphin and Ardagh; Tuam, Killala and Achonry. *Dublin:* Cashel and Ossory; Cork, Cloyne and Ross; Dublin and Glendalough; Limerick and Killaloe; Meath and Kildare.)
Geographical area: 32,000 square miles
Population: 4.5 million
Number of Anglicans: 400,000
Number of parishes: 450

Number of clergy: 500
Provincial mailing address:
Church of Ireland House
Church Avenue
Rathmines, Dublin, 6, Republic of Ireland

WEEK OF MARCH 23, 2003 *Lent 3*

GIVE THANKS for the Church of England.

Dioceses: 44 (*Canterbury*: Bath and Wells; Birmingham; Bristol; Canterbury; Chelmsford; Chichester; Coventry; Derby; Ely; Europe; Exeter; Gloucester; Guildford; Herford; Leicester; Lichfield; Lincoln; London; Norwich; Oxford; Peterborough; Portsmouth; Rochester; St. Albans; St. Edmundsbury and Ipswich; Salisbury; Southwark; Truro; Winchester; Worcester. *York:* Blackburn; Bradford; Carlisle; Chester; Durham; Liverpool; Manchester; Newcastle; Ripon and Leeds; Sheffield; Sodor and Man; Southwell; Wakefield; York)
Country: England
Population: 49,319,000
Number of parishes: 12,982
Number of clergy: 9,145
Provincial mailing address:
Lambeth Palace
London SE1 7JU
England

WEEK OF MARCH 30, 2003 *Lent 4*

GIVE THANKS for the Church of South India.

Countries: India, Sri Lanka

Dioceses: 21 (Chennai; Coimbatore; Dornakal; East Kerala; Jaffna; Kanyakumari; Karimnagar; Karnataka Central; Karnataka North; Karnataka South; Krishna-Godavari; Madhya Kerala; Madurai-Ramnad; Medak; Nandyal; North Kerala; Rayalaseema; South Kerala; Tirunelveli; Trichy-Tanjore; Vellore)

Provincial mailing address:

CSI Bishop's House
Diocese of East Kerala
Melukavumattom P.O.
Kottayam 686 652
Kerala State
India

WEEK OF APRIL 6, 2003 *Lent 5*

GIVE THANKS for the Episcopal Church of the Sudan.

Northern Sudan, once known as Nubia, was converted to Coptic Christianity in the 6th century. Arab conquests brought Islam in the 15th century. The Church Missionary Society arrived in 1899, in Omdurman in Northern Sudan, to find an overwhelmingly Muslim population. Their work spread Christianity rapidly among the black Africans of the South but in the primarily Arab north there was no such success. Until 1974, Sudan was a single diocese under the archbishop in Jerusalem. In 1974 it was divided into four dioceses with four bishops and became an independent Province. Since 1956 when Sudan became independent, the country and the church have suffered through a series of civil wars, violent persecutions of Christians and, in this decade, displacement of almost 5 million people. More than 1.5 million people were killed during the 1990s. Yet the church experiences explosive growth with some dioceses tripling in size every few years.

Dominant throughout the south, the Anglican Church has grown with amazing speed during the period of persecution. The Diocese of Bor's four congregations in 1984 had grown to 280 in 1997 and its faithful have produced 10,000 new hymns. Many of those new communicants are no longer in their homes. No one knows how many church members have been driven from the country. The Archbishop and his clergy cannot begin to meet the needs of those in displacement camps. Few others are even trying.

Yet the church continues to grow. And since all other institutions have been destroyed, the church now will have a crucial role in helping rebuild.

Country: Republic of the Sudan

Dioceses: 24 (Bor; Cueibet; El-Obeid; Ezzo; Ibba; Juba; Kadugli and Nuba Mountains; Kajokeji; Khartoum; Lainya; Lui; Malakal; Maridi; Mundri; Port Sudan; Rejaf; Renk; Rokon; Rumbeck; Torit; Wau; Yambio; Yei; Yirol)

Geographical area: 966,757 square miles

Population: 30,120,420

Number of Anglicans: 5,000,000

Other faiths: Muslims, 70+ percent; traditional belief, 10 percent
Number of clergy: 22 bishops, 2,923 clergy
Provincial mailing address:
P.O. Box 110,
Juba, Sudan

WEEK OF APRIL 13, 2003 *Sunday of the Passion: Palm Sunday*

GIVE THANKS for Jerusalem and the Middle East.

Dioceses: 4 (Cyprus and the Gulf; Egypt; Iran; Jerusalem)

WEEK OF APRIL 20, 2003 *Easter Day*

REJOICE NOW, heavenly hosts and choirs of angels, and let your trumpets shout Salvation for the victory of our mighty King.

Rejoice and sing now, all the round earth, bright with a glorious splendor, for darkness has been vanquished by our eternal King.

Rejoice and be glad now, Mother Church, and let your holy courts, in radiant light, resound with the praises of your people.

WEEK OF APRIL 27, 2003 *Easter 2*

GIVE THANKS for The Scottish Episcopal Church.

The Church in Scotland traces its history back to the earliest known Christian communities in Scotland about

400AD, maintaining that form of church order of bishops, priests and deacons.

In the late 1600s the reformed Church of Scotland broke in two. The story is complex. The Scottish Episcopal Church espoused the Jacobite cause and suffered the consequences. Though it has long since relinquished its Jacobite dreams it sadly remains separate from its sister church, the Church of Scotland (Presbyterian), though relationships with one another are happily cordial, with prayers that the break with Rome may be healed.

There, too, is much goodwill and cooperation as there is with the other churches in Scotland especially through its common membership of ACTS (Action of Churches Together in Scotland).

Country: Scotland
Geographical area: 1,750 square miles (approx.)
Population: 5,500,000 (approx.)
Number of Anglicans: 53,553
Number of Christians: 35 percent of population
Number of parishes: 320
Number of clergy: 420
Dioceses: 7 (Aberdeen and Orkney; Argyll and the Isles; Brechin; Edinburgh; Glasgow and Galloway; Moray, Ross, and Caithness; St. Andrews, Dunkeld, and Dunblane)
Provincial Address:
21 Grosvenor Crescent
Edinburgh, EH12 5EE
Scotland

WEEK OF MAY 4, 2003 *Easter 3*

Theological Education Sunday

PRAY for seminaries and schools of theology that train clergy and laity in the Christian faith.

WEEK OF MAY 11, 2003 *Easter 4*

GIVE THANKS for the Anglican Church of Korea.

The Province was founded on the 16th of April 1992.

Country: Korea
Dioceses: 3 (Pusan; Seoul; Taejon)
Geographical area: 81,000 square miles
Population: 65,000,000
Number of Anglicans: 15,000
Number of Christians: 13,000,000
Other faiths: Buddhism, Confucianism, Chun-do Kyo
Number of Parishes: 100
Number of Clergy: 120
Provincial mailing address:
3 Chong-Dong Chung-ku
Seoul 100-120
Republic of Korea

WEEK OF MAY 18, 2003 *Easter 5*

GIVE THANKS for the Church of the Province of Uganda.

The first missionaries to Uganda, Lt. Shergold Smith and the Rev. C.T. Wilson, arrived in June 1877. Five years later the first Anglican converts were baptized. Arab traders had bought Islam five years earlier. Roman Catholic missionaries arrived in 1879. Parties from the three religious groups stayed in the court of King Kabaka Mutesa, each trying to convert him. Their rivalry and hostility led to their failure. Mutesa died without being baptized. Mange, his son, turned against the Christians. Many were martyred. Yet, the more the king killed, the more came forward for baptism. The first Anglican cathedral, large enough to hold 4,000, was built in Namirembe in 1892. The first Ugandan clergy were ordained the next year. The Diocese of Uganda was established in 1897, carved out of the Diocese of Eastern Equatorial Africa. It became a separate Province in 1961. The East Africa Revival, which spread across a wide swath of the continent in the 1930s, found good soil in Uganda and continues today.

Uganda is a land that knows martyrdom...and knows God. Not only were some of the first missionaries murdered for insisting on their faith in this land locked nation in east Central Africa, so was the first bishop, James Hannington. In the last century, too, witness has been risky. Archbishop Janani Luwum lost his life in 1977, a victim of then President-for-Life Idi Amin, the evil tyrant, who allowed no opposition or criticism.

The church grew stronger under Amin, who was finally overthrown by Ugandan exiles with help from Tanzania in 1979.

In the past 10 years, the church has tripled in size. An archbishop house has been built which includes ample space for meetings and rooms for visitors.

Work has begun on upgrading and expanding the 100-year-old Bishop Tucker Theological College and attracting some of the academic staff from other parts of the communion.

Country: Republic of Uganda

Dioceses: 29 (Bukedi; Bunyoro; Busoga; Central Buganda; East Ankole; Kampala; Karamoja; Kigezi; Kinkizi; Kitgum; Kumi; Lango; Luwero; Madi and West Nile; Mbale; Mityana; Muhabura; Mukono; Namirembe; Nebbi; North Kigezi; North Mbale; Northern Uganda; Ruwenzori; Sebei; Soroti; South Rwenzori; West Ankole; West Buganda)

Geographical Area: 91,134 square miles

Population: 19,573,262

Number of Anglicans: 6,700,000

Christians: 89 percent (Roman Catholic 38 percent, Anglicans 34 percent)

Other faiths: Muslims 12 percent; traditional beliefs, other sects, 10 percent

Congregations: 1,731 parishes; 13,800 congregations

Clergy: 28 active bishops, 2,630 priests, 13,000 lay readers and catechists

Provincial mailing address:
PO Box 14123
Kampala, Uganda

WEEK OF MAY 25, 2003 *Easter 6*

Anglican Communion Sunday

PRAY for the Anglican Communion, the Anglican Consultative Council (ACC), for the Secretary General and the Anglican Communion Office staff.

The Anglican Communion has developed in two stages. Beginning in the 17th century, the Anglican Church was established by colonization in such countries as Australia, Canada, New Zealand, Southern Africa and the eastern part of the present U.S. Colonial bishoprics were set up under the authority of Canterbury in many parts of the British Empire; in other parts (e.g. North America) the Bishop of London exercised a distant supervision of local churches. After the American colonies achieved independence, the Episcopal Church in the USA became, in 1789, the first independent daughter church of the Church of England. The two churches were in full communion and had many informal relationships but no formal or legal ties, thus setting a pattern for the Anglican Communion of the future.

The second stage of development was the result of missionary expansion in the 19th and 20th centuries to other countries of Asia, Africa and Latin America and the formation of independent Provinces of the church in what was to become the British Commonwealth. The growth of autonomy in various branches of Anglicanism and the need for consultation led to the first Lambeth Conference in 1867.

WEEK OF JUNE 1, 2003 *Easter 7*

Anglican Communications Sunday

PRAY for the communication of the Gospel to all the World.

WEEK OF JUNE 8, 2003 *Pentecost*

PRAY for all church musicians: Organist-choirmasters, choristers, composers, musicians and small voices that give praise to God.

WEEK OF JUNE 15, 2003 *Trinity Sunday*

GIVE THANKS for the Anglican Church of Papua New Guinea.

The province was founded in 1977.

Countries: Papua New Guinea

Dioceses: 5 (Aipo Rongo; Dogura; New Guinea Islands; Port Moresby; Popondota)

Population: 4,000,000

Number of Anglicans: 140,000

Number of Christians: 3,800,000

Other faiths: Animism in remote areas

Number of parishes: 126

Number of clergy: 127

Provincial mailing address:

P.O. Box 673
Lae Morobe Province
Papua New Guinea

WEEK OF JUNE 22, 2003 *2 Pentecost*

GIVE THANKS for the Church in Pakistan.

Country: Pakistan

Dioceses: 9 (Arabian Gulf; Faisalabad; Hyderabad; Karachi; Lahore; Multan; Peshawar; Raiwind; Sialkot)

Provincial mailing address:
17 Warris Road
P.O. Box 2319
Lahore 3, Pakistan

WEEK OF JUNE 29, 2003 *3 Pentecost*

GIVE THANKS for the Anglican Church of the Central American Region (La Iglesia Anglicana de la Región Central de America [IARCA]).

On the 18th of April 1998 the Anglican Church of Central American became an autonomous Province. The origins of the Episcopal Churches in Central America and Panama have their base in the Church of England and the Episcopal Church of the United States. In the eighteenth century, England had two colonies in Central America, Belize and Miskitia, occupying a region between Nicaragua and Honduras. The natives of this region were evangelized mainly by the Church of England through missionary societies, in particular the Evangelical Propagation Society.

From the 19th century the United States has had economic interests in Central America, although its consolidation, influence, and commercial monopoly came after WWII. The construction of the Panama Canal promoted a strong presence of the Episcopal Church of the USA. This created the Missionary Diocese of the Canal Zone in 1919.

In January 1947 jurisdiction was transferred from the Church of England to the Episcopal Church for the chaplaincies of Nicaragua, Costa Rica, Bocas del Toro and Chiriqui in Panama and the north of Columbia. In

1956 Honduras, Guatemala and El Salvador transferred. This formed the Missionary District of the Episcopal Church in Central America in 1957, formed by the existing churches in Guatemala, El Salvador, Nicaragua, and Costa Rica.

Until 1957, the Episcopal/Anglican presence in Central America was set up in chapels that tended to immigrants and their descendants. There was no pastoral evangelization for the Central American natives, nor was there any interest to create national or local churches with the local culture.

With the support of the Lambeth Conferences in 1958 and 1968, however, there was an effort in Central America to change from a chapel system (strangers in a foreign land) to an indigenous, national and autonomous church. As a result, in 1967 the missionary dioceses of Guatemala, Honduras, El Salvador, Nicaragua and Costa Rica were created, with the purpose of extending the kingdom of God in each nation, and to present the Anglican Spirit in the local culture and form a native Anglican Church.

IARCA (la Iglesia Anglicana de la Región Central de America) has established a financial and program covenant with the Episcopal Church. This covenant contemplates the development of a financial plan and a forty-year appropriation reduction. This financial project implies a gradual reduction process for subsidies and growth from the diocesan contribution for the budget that will allow the sustained development of the Church's ministry.

Countries: Costa Rica, El Salvador, Guatemala, Nicaragua, Panama

Dioceses: 5 (Costa Rica; El Salvador; Guatemala; Nicaragua; Panama)
Provincial mailing address:
Iglesia Episcopal Costarricense
Apartado 2773
1000 San Jose, Costa Rica

WEEK OF JULY 6, 2003 *4 Pentecost*

GIVE THANKS for the Church of North India.

Country: India
Dioceses: 26 (Agra; Amritsar; Andaman and Car Nicobar Islands; Barrackpore; Bhopal; Calcutta; Chandigarh; Chotanagpur; Cuttack; Delhi; Durgapur; Eastern Himalayas; Gujarat; Jabalpur; Kolhapur; Lucknow; Marathwada; Mumbai (formerly Bombay); Nagpur; Nasik; North East India; Patna; Phulbani; Pune; Rajasthan; Sambalpur)
Provincial mailing address:
Cathedral House
Civil Lines
Sadar, Nagpur 440 001
Maharashtra
India

WEEK OF JULY 13, 2003 *5 Pentecost*

GIVE THANKS for the Church of Bangladesh.

The Province was founded in 1971. Only 0.3 percent of the people in Bangladesh are Christian. There is a theological college in Dhaka for training young people for ministry.

Bangladesh needs more presbyters and financial assistance for the children's education programme (37 primary schools) and for training in and development of the schools.

This is a low-lying disaster prone country which faces many natural calamities almost every year. People are poor and illiterate and depend mostly on agriculture. In order to achieve self-reliance, a social development program is involved in community development, income-generation, adult literacy, social forestry, vocational training, group formation savings and credit, youth development, women's development, schools, hospitals, community health and nutrition.

Country: Bangladesh
Dioceses: 2 (Dhaka; Kushtia)
Geographical area: 55,126 square miles
Population: 128.25 million
Number of Anglicans: 13,000
Number of Christians: 350,000
Other faiths: Islam (Muslim) 87 percent; Hindu 12 percent; Buddhist, Christian, etc. 1 percent
Number of parishes: 50
Number of clergy: 24
Provincial mailing address:
St. Thomas' Church
54 Johnson Road
Dhaka, 1100 Bangladesh

GIVE THANKS for the Church of Nigeria (Anglican Communion).

In the middle of the 19th century, freed Christian slaves from Sierra Leone arrived in Nigeria bringing Christianity with them. At about the same time, Church Missionary Society (CMS) missionary Henry Townsend and Methodist Thomas Birch Freeman entered the country and, on Christmas Day 1842, celebrated Eucharist under an agia tree in Badagri on the coast near Lagos. By 1857, CMS had established its Nigeria Mission and started working in from the coast, planting churches, schools and an evangelist ministry. They encountered considerable resistance. Converts were expelled from their villages. Christian men were flogged, had their homes burned, their land, property and wives confiscated. About 100 years later (1951) the province of West Africa was born, including all of Nigeria, Ghana and several other countries. Nigeria became an independent Province in 1979 and divided into three provinces on October 3, 1997.

The Decade of Evangelism prompted a daring and forceful act in the Province of Nigeria: the sending of 13 newly commissioned missionary bishops into the country's Muslim-dominated and hostile north, an area previously neglected by the church. Since 1900, when Lord Frederick Lugard, a British colonial governor trying to keep peace, proclaimed all territory from Lokoja north "blocked to the Gospel," the northern two thirds of Nigeria has heard scant Christian preaching. Relatively few churches had been established. That all changed in

January 1990. The church "unblocked" the Gospel by consecrating eight bishops and sending them off to pre-drawn dioceses. They were paid by parishes in the capital city, Lagos. The venture has been successful in every diocese, but in some, progress has been phenomenal.

Evangelism in this land of diverse peoples must conquer the challenge of language. Nigerian citizens speak 350 different languages. There are, however, three major ones—Hausa, Yoruba and Ibo. Inculturating the faith in the Nigerian context will also help and the church is about that task by making sure that whatever spirituality there is in traditional religion is brought into the church, knowing that it is okay to praise the Lord with drums and dancing.

Country: Federal Republic of Nigeria

Dioceses: 78 (*Province I:* Akoko; Akure; Benin; Egba; Ekiti; Ekiti West; Ibadan; Ibadan North; Ibadan South; Ife; Igbomina; Ijebu; Ikale-Ilaje; Ilesa; Kabba; Kwara; Lagos; Lagos West; Lokoja; Offa; Oke-Osun; Ondo; Osun; Owo; Remo; Sabongidda-Ora; Ughelli; Warri; Yewa (Egbado). *Province II:* Aba; Abakaliki; Asaba; Awka; Calabar; Egbu; Enugu; Esan; Ideato; Ikka; Mbaise; The Niger Delta; Niger Delta North; Niger Delta West; Nnewi; Nsukka; Oji River; Okigwe North; Okigwe South; Oleh; On the Niger; Orlu; Owerri; Ukwa; Umuahia; Uyo. *Province III:* Abuja; Bauchi; Bida; Damaturu; Dutse; Gombe; Gusau; Gwagwalada; Jalingo; Jos; Kaduna; Kafanchan; Kano; Katsina; Kebbi; Lafia; Maiduguri; Makurdi; Minna; Oturkpo; Sokoto; Wusasa; Yola)

Geographical area: 356,669 square miles
Population: 103,912,489
Anglicans: 14 percent
Christians: 50 percent (Roman Catholics, 12 percent; Pentecostals and other Protestants, 23 percent)
Other faiths: Muslims, 43 percent; Traditional beliefs, 5 percent
Congregations: 3,680 parishes; 5,000+ congregations
Clergy: approximately 4,000
Provincial Office:
Provincial Secretariat
29 Marina
P.O. Box 78
Lagos, Nigeria

WEEK OF JULY 27, 2003 *7 Pentecost*

GIVE THANKS for the Church of the Southern Cone (Iglesia Anglicana del Cono Sur de America).

Countries: Argentina, Bolivia, Chile, Paraguay, Peru, Uruguay
Dioceses: 7 (Argentina; Bolivia; Chile; Northern Argentina; Paraguay; Peru; Uruguay)
Provincial mailing address:
Bishop of Northern Argentina
Church of the Southern Cone
Iglesia Anglicana, Casilla de Correo 187
4400 Salta, Argentina

WEEK OF AUGUST 3, 2003 *8 Pentecost*

GIVE THANKS for the extra-provincial Episcopal Church of Cuba (Iglesia Episcopal de Cuba).

WEEK OF AUGUST 10, 2003 *9 Pentecost*

GIVE THANKS for the Province of Melanesia.

Countries: New Caledonia, Solomon Islands, Vanuatu
Dioceses: 8 (Banks and Torres; Central Melanesia; Central Solomons; Hanuato'o; Malaita; Temotu; Vanuatu; Ysabel)
Provincial mailing address:
Church of Melanesia
P.O. Box 19
Honiara, Solomon Islands

WEEK OF AUGUST 17, 2003 *10 Pentecost*

THANK GOD for the generosity of those who give abundantly of their time, talent and treasure for the spread of the Kingdom of God.

WEEK OF AUGUST 24, 2003 *11 Pentecost*

GIVE THANKS for the Church of the Province of West Africa.

The first Christian missionaries, Portuguese Roman Catholics, came to the Gold Coast, now Ghana, in 1482. The first Anglican missionary arrived in 1752, the Rev. Thomas Thompson from the Society for the Propagation of the Gospel. Thompson sent three Ghanian converts back to Britain to be trained. One survived. Philip Qarcoe, the first Ghanian priest, returned to start a ministry with the mulatto offspring of expatriots. An intensive phase of evangelization began in the late 19th century. Five dioceses were formed into the Province of West Africa in 1951. The first indigenous bishop, I. Lamaire, was elected to lead the Diocese of Accra in 1968. He later became the first indigenous Archbishop.

Evangelism paired with development is changing lives in the six countries that make up the Province of West Africa. Many have initiated programs to expand food production and offer primary health care in addition to the elementary schools that almost every church provides. A farm owned and operated by the Diocese of Koforidua in Ghana creates employment, produces food and generates income for the church.

Countries: Cameroon, Ghana, Guinea, Liberia, Sierra Leone, The Gambia

Geographical area: 262,086 square miles

Population: 45,000,000

Christians: 10,000,000 +

Other faiths: Muslim 25 percent (Ghana) to 95 percent (Gambia) depending on country; traditional religions 23 percent or higher depending on country; unspecified 20 to 30 percent

Anglicans: 1,000,000 +

Dioceses: 13 (Accra; Bo; Cameroon (Region Missionaire); Cape Coast; Freetown; Gambia; Guinea; Koforidua; Kumasi; Liberia; Sekondi; Sunyani; Tamale)

Congregations: 600 parishes

Clergy: 450
Provincial Office:
P.O. Box 8
Accra, Ghana

WEEK OF AUGUST 31, 2003 *12 Pentecost*

GIVE THANKS for the Anglican Church in Aotearoa, New Zealand and Polynesia.

The Anglican Church in Aotearoa, New Zealand and Polynesia, with its beginnings in 1814, is made up of several Pacific Island nations in addition to New Zealand. It is a three Tikanga (custom, criterion) church, seeking to be faithful as a people of God within three cultural streams—Maori, Pakeha and Polynesian. Each part of the church has equal autonomy, status and respect, and is bound together by a common constitution and mission statement. Within the Pacific Islands it is a minority church where traditional values and customs regarding church life are preserved. Within Aotearoa, New Zealand, it is one of the major churches.

Countries: Aotearoa, New Zealand, Fiji, Tonga, and Samoa
Dioceses: 9 (Aotearoa; Auckland; Christchurch; Dunedin; Nelson; Polynesia; Waiapu; Waikato; Wellington)
Provincial mailing address:
P.O. Box 885
Hastings New Zealand

GIVE THANKS for the Episcopal Church of the United States of America.

The Episcopal Church has its beginnings with the Church of England, formed early in Britain when, in order to resist the encroachments and claims of the papacy, the English Church broke from Rome in the 1500s.

The Episcopal Church came to America when English colonists arrived in what is now the U.S. They brought the church with them and began to organize its temporal affairs at the same time that the government was beginning to take form.

Missionaries sent by the English Society for the Propagation of the Gospel in Foreign Parts were responsible for much of the work of the Church in the colonies. The church held its first General Convention in 1785, and spread with the pioneers into the Northwest and to the coast of California in covered wagons with the early settlers. During the Civil War, the Episcopal Church was divided; but the Church repaired its divisions after the War and, beginning with the General Convention of 1865, northern and southern bishops and deputies met together as before. The Episcopal Church has since spread the Christian faith and its unique blend of catholic and protestant theology and liturgy throughout its congregations.

Countries: The United States of America, Columbia, Dominican Republic, Ecuador, Haiti, Honduras, Taiwan, Virgin Islands
Dioceses: 109; Provinces: 9
Geographical area: 3,526,278 square miles

Population: 287,731,000
Number of Episcopalians: 2,409,155
Other faiths: Judaism, Islam, Hindu, and others.
Number of parishes: 7,403
Number of clergy: 15,130
Provincial mailing address:

Episcopal Church Center
815 Second Ave.
New York, NY 10017
USA

WEEK OF SEPTEMBER 14, 2003 *14 Pentecost*

We continue this week our prayers for The Episcopal Church, the United States of America.

WEEK OF SEPTEMBER 21, 2003 *15 Pentecost*

GIVE THANKS for the Anglican Church of Canada (L'Eglise Anglicane du Canada).

The first Anglican Communion service in what is now Canada took place on 22 July 1578 aboard the ship "Judith" in the waters near Baffin Island. It was celebrated by the English priest, Robert Wolfall. Settlement and church growth in Canada began to flourish from the mid-eighteenth century onward. The Anglican episcopate in Canada began in 1787 with the consecration of Charles Inglis as Bishop of Nova Scotia. The first General Synod (i.e. national legislative body) of the Canadian Church met in 1893. General Synod now meets every three years and comprises the archbishops, bishops, and elected clergy and lay representatives of all thirty dioceses. The church is organized into four internal ecclesiastical provinces, each with an elected metropolitan archbishop. The work of General Synod is carried out between sessions under the authority of the Council of General Synod which meets twice a year.

The Anglican Church of Canada serves in a diverse and rapidly-changing Canada. The multicultural face of Canada is increasingly reflected in church membership, and the church's worship life increasingly shows signs of the riches brought into its life from around the world. Within that diversity, church members who are also members of Canada's First Nations are establishing a renewed presence (New Agape) within the Anglican Church of Canada. The Anglican Church of Canada celebrates its heritage at the same time as it comes to terms with some of the consequences of its past. Challenges abound as we look to the future and our role in shaping it.

Country: Canada

Dioceses: 30 (*British Columbia*: British Columbia; Caledonia; Anglican Parishes of the Central Interior (formerly Cariboo); Kootenay; New Westminster; Yukon. *Canada*: Central Newfoundland; Eastern Newfoundland and Labrador; Fredericton; Montreal; Nova Scotia and Prince Edward Island; Quebec; Western Newfoundland. *Rupert's Land*: The Arctic; Athabasca; Brandon; Calgary; Edmonton; Keewatin; Qu'Appelle; Rupert's Land; Saskatchewan; Saskatoon. *Ontario*: Algoma; Huron; Moosonee; Niagara; Ontario; Ottawa; Toronto)

Geographical area: 9,970,610 square kilometres
Population: 29.6 million
Number of Census Anglicans: 2,188,110
Number of Christians: 22,503,360
Other faiths: 1,093,680
Number of parishes: 1,793; Congregations: 2,836
Number of clergy: 3,517
Provincial mailing address:
600 Jarvis Street
Toronto ON Canada M4Y 2J6
www.anglican.ca

WEEK OF SEPTEMBER 28, 2003 *16 Pentecost*

GIVE THANKS for the Church of Nippon Sei Ko Kai (The Anglican Communion in Japan).

In early 1859 while Japan was still closed to other nations, the first two foreign missionaries entered Japan at Nagasaki and lived there quietly learning and studying and being open to people. They were sent by the Episcopal Church USA as a result of the visits to Japan by Commodore Perry and the first Consul, Townsend Harris, both Episcopalians. Of the two clergymen, Mr. Liggins was soon to leave for medical reasons, but Channing Moore Williams was bound to remain in Japan until 1910 and during that time to become the Bishop of China and Japan, Bishop of Edo, founder of many institutions and churches, and the founding father of the Nippon Sei Ko Kai. He was soon joined in his beginning work by missionaries sent by the Church of England from the Church Missionary Scoiety (CMS) and Society for the

Propagation of the Gospel (SPG), then by the Church of Canada, and the Church of Australia. So the NSKK has a rich heritage and polychrome background of Anglicanism. In 1877 the NSKK was officially formed as a legal religious body, and began the long process towards autonomous leadership and support. The first Japanese bishop was consecrated in 1923 when the Diocese of Tokyo was formed as a self-supporting diocese, immediately followed by a bishop for the new Diocese of Osaka. At the beginning of the Pacific War, all of the bishops of the dioceses were Japanese and the church was driven into a period of persecution and dispersion because NSKK did not join the United Church by government order. The end of the war found the church with much loss of life and destroyed property but a spirit of new beginning and a new-found unity. With assistance from its overseas sister churches the work began and today all NSKK dioceses have a Japanese bishop. There are 15 expatriate missionaries from partner churches serving in NSKK.

Country: Japan

Dioceses: 11 (Chubu; Hokkaido; Kita Kanto; Kobe; Kyoto; Kyushu; Okinawa; Osaka; Tohoku; Tokyo; Yokohama)

Geographical area: 370,000 square kilometers

Population: 125,300,000

Number of Anglicans: 57,407

Number of Christians: 1,063,663

Other faiths: Shinto, Buddhist

Number of Parishes: 318

Number of Clergy: 348

Provincial mailing address:
Nippon Sei Ko Kai Provincial Office
65-3 Yarai Cho
Shinjuku-ku, Tokyo 162-0805
Japan

WEEK OF OCTOBER 5, 2003 *17 Pentecost*

GIVE THANKS for the Church in the Province of the West Indies.

Countries: Antigua, Aruba, Bahamas, Barbados, Belize, Guyana, Jamaica, Tabago, Trinidad, Windward Islands
Dioceses: 8 (Barbados; Belize; Guyana; Jamaica; Nassau and the Bahamas; North Eastern Caribbean and Aruba; Trinidad and Tobago; Windward Islands)
Provincial mailing address:
Church in the Province of the West Indies
PO Box N-7107
Nassau, Bahamas

WEEK OF OCTOBER 12, 2003 *18 Pentecost*

GIVE THANKS for the province of York in the Church of England.

The Northern province of the Church of England comprises parishes in towns and cities formed by the industrial revolution as well as in deeply rural areas. It was a meeting place for the Celtic and Roman church and has produced remarkable saints: St. Aidan, St. Hilda, St. Paulinus, St. Cuthbert and St. Caedmon, among others.

Country: England
Geographical area: 15,414
Population: 15,332,000
Other faiths: Islam, Hinduism; Buddhism; Judaism; Sikhism
Dioceses: 14 (Blackburn; Bradford; Carlisle; Chester; Durham; Liverpool; Manchester; Newcastle; Ripon and Leeds; Sheffield; Sodor and Man; Southwell; Wakefield; York)
Parishes: 3,182
Clergy: 2,945
Provincial Office:
Bishopthorpe Palace
Bishopthorpe, York
North Yorks YO2 1QE
England

WEEK OF OCTOBER 19, 2003 *19 Pentecost*

GIVE THANKS for the Anglican Church of Tanzania.

Universities Mission to Central Africa began work in Zanzibar and what was then Tanganyika in 1864. Young evangelists from England's four major universities came in response to explorer-missionary David Livingstone's appeal to continue his work. Malaria was unknown at the time and many of the young graduates never went home. Their graves fill the ground of the early mission stations. The Church Missionary Society arrived in 1878. The center of their mission work was at Mpwapwa, about 180 miles in from the coast where missionaries established a way station on the route to Uganda. One of the first converts, Peter Nemo is still remembered. Sent to Britain for training, he returned and evangelized the whole area. In 1970, the nine dioceses in Tanzania and Zanzibar left the Province of East Africa to become the Province of Tanzania.

Islam is on the march in the Province of Tanzania. The church is witnessing an aggressive campaign both on Zanzibar, the Isle of Cloves just off the coast, and on the mainland where Tanzania stretches between Kenya and Mozambique. Islam has been present on the Isle of Zanzibar and in Tanzania much longer than Christianity, 800 years longer. The first Arab traders and slavers began their operations in the 8th Century. For several hundred years, Zanzibar was the center for Arab slave-traders. The Portuguese and other Europeans didn't arrive until the 1500s. In response, most diocese are making evangelism a priority with some good results. Some Muslims are being converted, but such conversions come at a cost. Becoming Christian can mean losing family and acceptance in the community.

Countries: United Republic of Tanzania (includes Island of Zanzibar)

Dioceses: 19 (Central Tanganyika; Dar-es Salaam; Kagera; Kondoa; Mara; Masasi; Morogoro; Mount Kilimanjaro; Mpwapwa; Rift Valley; Ruaha; Ruvuma; South West Tanganyika; Southern Highlands; Tabora; Tanga; Victoria Nyanza; Western Tanganyika; Zanzibar)

Geographical area: 363,708

Population: 30,000,000

Number of Anglicans: About 2 million

Number of Christians: 45 percent

Other faiths: Muslims, 35 percent; Traditional beliefs, 15 percent; Other 5 percent

Number of clergy: 16 bishops, 685 priests and deacons
Provincial mailing address:
P.O. Box 899
Dodoma
Tanzania

WEEK OF OCTOBER 26, 2003 *20 Pentecost*

GIVE THANKS for the Church of South East Asia.

Countries: Brunei, Cambodia, Indonesia, Laos, Malaysia, Singapore, Thailand, Vietnam
Dioceses: 4 (Kuching; Sabah; Singapore; West Malaysia)
Population: 350,000,000
Provincial mailing address:
PO Box 10811
88809 Koto Kinabalu
Sabah
Malaysia

WEEK OF NOVEMBER 2, 2003 *21 Pentecost*

GIVE THANKS for the Church in Wales.

Country: Wales
Dioceses: 6 (St. Asaph; Bangor; St. David's; Llandaff; Swansea and Brecon; Monmouth)
Geographical area: 8,019 square miles
Population: 2,900,000
Number of Anglicans: 95,000
Number of parishes: 578
Number of clergy: 765

Provincial mailing address:
39 Cathedral Road
Cardiff, South Glamorgan CF1 9XF
Wales

WEEK OF NOVEMBER 9, 2003 *22 Pentecost*

GIVE THANKS for the Province of the Anglican Church of Congo (Province de L'Eglise Anglicane du Congo).

The Anglican Church was established in Congo in 1896 by Canon Apolo Kivebulaya, an evangelist from Uganda who was based in Boga-Zaire (now Congo). In 1954 the Anglican Church was able to reach the Shaba (now Katanga) region, but it was not until the 1970s that large parts of Congo were evangelised.

Following independence, the Church began to expand and form dioceses as part of the Province of Uganda, Burundi, Rwanda and Boga-Zaire. During the Partners in Mission Consultation held in Kigali in 1989, it was proposed that Zaire should form a new Province. This was approved by the Anglican Consultative Council. The new Province celebrated the Centenary of the Anglican Church in Congo.

Country: Democratic Republic of Congo
Dioceses: 6 (Boga; Bukavu; Kisangani; Katanga; Nord-Kivu; Kindu)
Geographical area: 2,345,409 square kilometers
Population: 45,000,000
Number of Anglicans: 160,000

Other faiths and denominations: Roman Catholic, Protestant churches, African Indigenous churches, Orthodox, Jews and Sunni Muslims.
Number of parishes: 241
Number of clergy: 270
Provincial mailing address:
Province of the Anglican Church
of Congo/Bunia
P.O. Box 25586
Kampala, Uganda

WEEK OF NOVEMBER 16, 2003 *23 Pentecost*

GIVE THANKS for the extra-provincial Dioceses of Puerto Rico, Venezuela, and the Falkland Islands; the extra-provincial Lusitanian Church of Portugal; and the Spanish Reformed Episcopal Church.

WEEK OF NOVEMBER 23, 2003 *Last Pentecost: Christ the King*

GIVE THANKS for the Episcopal Anglican Church of Brazil (Igreaja Episcopal Anglicana Do Brasil).

The starting of the Brazilian mission belongs to the students of the Virginia Theological Seminary. James Watson Morris and Lucien Lee Kinsolving arrived in 1889. Just one year after their appointment, on Trinity Sunday, June 1, 1890, the first service was held in the parlor of their rented house where they had improvised a crude chapel. In the following years came three more American missionaries: John Gaw Meem, William Cabell Brown and Mary Packard. Since then the missionary work has developed in such a way that the church transformed herself into an autonomous province of the Anglican Communion in 1965.

Country: Brazil

Dioceses: 7 (Brasilia; Pelotas; Recife; Rio de Janeiro; São Paulo; Southern Brazil; Southwestern Brazil)

Geographical area: 8,547,403 km2

Population: 155,822,440

Number of Anglicans: 42,670 (communicants), 103,021 (baptised)

Number of clergy: 131

Provincial mailing address:
Caixa Postal 11 510
Porto Alegre, RS, 91720-150
Brazil

WEEK OF November 30, 2003 *Advent 1*

GIVE THANKS for the Anglican Church of Kenya.

Country: Kenya

Dioceses: 26 (Bondo; Bungoma; Butere; Eldoret; Embu; Kajiado; Katakwa; Kirinyaga; Kitale; Kitui; Machakos; Maseno North; Maseno South; Maseno West; Mbeere; Meru; Mombasa; Mount Kenya Central; Mount Kenya South; Mount Kenya West; Nairobi; Nakuru; Nambale; Nyahururu; Taita-Taveta; Thika)

Provincial mailing address:
P. O. Box 40502
Nairobi, Kenya

GIVE THANKS for the Episcopal Church in the Philippines (Iglesia Episkopal sa Philipinas).

The Episcopal Church in the Philippines is an Autonomous Church and a Church Province in the Anglican Communion. It began in 1901 as the Missionary District of the Philippines in the Episcopal Church in the United States of America (ECUSA). On May 1, 1990 it was inaugurated as an Autonomous Province in the Anglican Communion with the name: The Episcopal Church in the Philippines.

The first bishop of this Church was Charles Henry Brent—a great ecumenist and a great spokesman for the missionary case, social concerns and the Faith and Order Movement. As an ecumenist, he did not sign the Comity Agreement which divided the country as missionary areas of the various religious groups outside the Roman Catholic Church. Instead, he established and began his District in areas where there were no Christians. This explains why up to this time the predominant members of this Church are from the minority tribes.

Brent's Philippine Missionary Policy centered on the consciousness that the mission of the Episcopal Church should be to preach the Gospel in areas where there is no active work of other Christian bodies. Finding the Roman Catholic Church already active and in widespread existence in the country, Bishop Brent rejected proselytizing as a strategy for mission and adopted one of "not putting an altar over and against another altar." Bishop Brent targeted three major areas for mission: 1) The unchurched Chinese and growing Caucasian population in Manila; 2) The native Muslims and pagan tribes in Mindanao who were not subjugated by Spain nor converted to Christianity; and 3) The fierce pagan tribes of Northern Luzon who were also not subjugated by Spain nor converted to Christianity.

Country: Philippines
Dioceses: 6 (Central Philippines; North Central Philippines; Northern Luzon; Northern Philippines; Santiago; Southern Philippines)
Geographical area: 300,439 square kilometers
Population: 65 million
Number of Anglicans: 118,714
Other faiths: Muslim
Number of Parishes: 1,042
Number of Clergy: 252
Provincial mailing address:
P.O. Box 10321
Broadway Centrum
Quezon City, 1112 Philippines

WEEK OF DECEMBER 14, 2003 *Advent 3*

GIVE THANKS for the Church of the Province of Southern Africa.

The Church of the Province of South Africa is focusing on transformation and believes that in order to attain genuine transformation it must be owned by the people rather than be dominated by clericalism. To this end, then, the CPSA is involved in consultations and workshops on change at the local church level, parish level, archdeaconry level, diocesan level and provincial level.

CPSA is also focusing on the African continent. For the South Africans particularly this is very important. Before, South Africa knew more about the United Kingdom and the United States of America than Africa. The first meeting of the African archbishops took place in July 1997 in Johannesburg. There is a great need for inculturation in all spheres of life. We now have a Standing Commission on African Culture and Christianity which reports to the Synod of Bishops.

The province recently celebrated the 150th anniversary of the arrival of Bishop Robert Gray, first bishop of Cape Town, in 1847.

Countries: South Africa, Lesotho, Swaziland, Angola, Mozambique, Namibia, St. Helena, Ascension Island

Dioceses: 23 (Angola (Missionary Diocese); Bloemfontein; Cape Town; Christ the King; George; Grahamstown; Highveld; Johannesburg; Kimberley and Kuruman; Klerksdorp; Lebombo; Lesotho; Namibia; Natal; Niassa; Port Elizabeth; Pretoria; St. Helena; St. John's; St. Mark the Evangelist; Swaziland; Umzimvubu; Zululand)

Geographical area: 4,276,993 square kilometres

Population: 80,700,000

Number of Anglicans: 3,000,000

Number of Christians: 28,500,000

Other faiths: African Traditional, Hindu, Moslem, Buddhist

Number of parishes: 994 (approximately 1900 congregations)

Number of clergy: 1,240
Provincial mailing address:
16-20 Bishopscourt Drive
Bishopscourt
Claremont, 7708 South Africa

WEEK OF DECEMBER 21, 2003 *Advent 4*

GIVE THANKS for the gift of God's Incarnate Son to be the Saviour and Redeemer of the world.

PRAY for the Church of God throughout the world.

WEEK OF DECEMBER 28, 2003 *Christmas 1*

GIVE THANKS for the Church of Ceylon.

Country: Sri Lanka
Dioceses: 2 (Colombo; Kurunagala)
Mailing address:
Bishop's House
368/2 Buaddhaloka
Mawatha Columbo 7
Sri Lanka

Anglican Cycle of Prayer

A Daily Guide for the Year of Our Lord 2003

Anglican Cycle of Prayer

A daily guide for the Year of Our Lord 2003

Wednesday—January 1: *Holy Name.*

PRAYfor another year of Grace.

ETERNAL FATHER, you gave to your incarnate Son the holy name of Jesus to be the sign of our salvation: Plant in every heart, we pray, the love of him who is the Savior of the world, our Lord Jesus Christ; who lives and reigns with you and the Holy Spirit, one God, in glory everlasting. Amen.

Thursday—2: GIVE THANKS for the extra-provincial **Diocese of Bermuda.** (Canterbury, *England*)

Friday—3: Europe. (Canterbury, *England*)

Saturday—4: Convocation of American Churches in Europe. (Province II, *The Episcopal Church U.S.*)

WEEK OF JANUARY 5, 2003 *Christmas 2*

GIVE THANKS for the Church of Myanmar (formerly Burma).

PRAY for peace, justice and democracy.

Monday—6: *The Epiphany.*

PRAY for the people and clergy of the diocese of **Hpa-an.** *(Myanmar)*

Tuesday—7: Mandalay. *(Myanmar)*

Wednesday—8: Mytikyina. *(Myanmar)*

Thursday—9: Sittwe. *(Myanmar)*

Friday—10: Toungoo. *(Myanmar)*

Saturday—11: Yangon. *(Myanmar)*

WEEK OF JANUARY 12, 2003 *1 Epiphany: The Baptism of Our Lord*

GIVE THANKS for the Anglican Church of Australia.

Monday—13: The Murray; Adelaide; Willochra. (South Australia, *Australia)*

Tuesday—14: Bunbury; North West Australia; Perth. (Western Australia, *Australia)*

Wednesday—15: Armidale; Bathurst; Canberra and Goulburn; Grafton; Newcastle; Riverina; Sydney. (New South Wales, *Australia)*

Thursday—16: Brisbane; North Queensland; The Northern Territory; Rockhampton. (Queensland, *Australia)*

Friday—17: Ballarat; Bendigo; Gippsland; Melbourne, Wangaratta. (Victoria, *Australia)*

Saturday—18: *The Confession of St. Peter.*

Tasmania, Australia. *(Extra-provincial)*

WEEK OF JANUARY 19, 2003 *2 Epiphany*

Week of Prayer for Christian Unity

PRAY for the World Council of Churches and all institutions and organizations promoting Christian unity and for the healing of all schisms within the One, Holy, Catholic and Apostolic Church.

Monday—20: PRAY for the Orthodox churches in communion with the Patriarch of Constantinople.

Tuesday—21: PRAY for all churches in communion with the Bishop of Rome.

Wednesday—22: PRAY for the Coptic, Oriental Orthodox, and other autonomous and independent churches.

Thursday—23: PRAY for churches whose roots are in the protestant reformation.

Friday—24: PRAY for churches in communion with the Churches of the Anglican Communion.

Saturday—25: *The Conversion of St. Paul.*

PRAY for all churches in dialogue with the churches of the Anglican Communion.

WEEK OF JANUARY 26, 2003 *3 Epiphany*

The Archbishop of Canterbury

ALMIGHTY and everlasting God, from whom cometh every good and perfect gift: Send down upon the Archbishop of Canterbury, the healthful Spirit of thy grace; and that he may continually please thee, pour upon him the continual dew of thy blessing. Grant this, O Lord, for the honour of our Advocate and Mediator, Jesus Christ. Amen.

PRAY for the work, ministry and witness of the Archbishop of Canterbury, Rowan D. Williams.

Monday—27: PRAY for the Anglican Primates, the chief bishop of every Church in the Communion.

Tuesday—28: PRAY for Canterbury Cathedral and Centre.

Wednesday—29: PRAY for the Anglican Observer at the United Nations.

Thursday—30: PRAY for Interfaith conversations between Anglicans and other faiths.

Friday—31: PRAY for the Networks and Commissions of the Anglican Communion.

Saturday—February 1: PRAY for the Compass Rose Society.

WEEK OF FEBRUARY 2, 2003 *The Presentation of Our Lord—Candlemas*

GIVE THANKS for the Province of the Indian Ocean (Provansa Eklesiastikan'ny Oseana Indiana) (Province Ecclesiastique De L'Ocean Indien).

Monday—3: Antananarivo, Madagascar. (*Indian Ocean*)

Tuesday—4: Antsiranana, Madagascar. (*Indian Ocean*)

Wednesday—5: Fianarantsoa; Mahajanga. (*Indian Ocean*)

Thursday—6: Mauritius. (*Indian Ocean*)

Friday—7: Seychelles. (*Indian Ocean)*

Saturday—8: Toamasina. (*Indian Ocean*)

WEEK OF FEBRUARY 9, 2003 *5 Epiphany*

GIVE THANKS for the Church of the Province of Burundi.

PRAY for the restoration of justice, peace, and reconciliation.

Monday—10: Bujumbura. *(Burundi)*

Tuesday—11: Buye. *(Burundi)*

Wednesday—12: Gitega. *(Burundi)*

Thursday—13: Makamba. *(Burundi)*

Friday—14: Matana. *(Burundi)*

Saturday—15: PRAY for physicians, dentists, nurses and healthcare workers who give of themselves to treat the poor.

WEEK OF FEBRUARY 16, 2003 *6 Epiphany*

GIVE THANKS for the Province of Hong Kong Sheng Kung Hui.

Monday—17: Eastern Kowloon. *(Hong Kong Sheng Kung Hui)*

Tuesday—18: Hong Kong Island. *(Hong Kong Sheng Kung Hui)*

Wednesday—19: Western Kowloon. *(Hong Kong Sheng Kung Hui)*

Thursday—20: PRAY for the brotherhood of the human family, and for the end of racism.

Friday—21: PRAY for those who serve on parish vestries and mission committees for the good of the local parish.

Saturday—22: PRAY for those who serve on Diocesan or Provincial commissions and committees.

WEEK OF FEBRUARY 23, 2003 *7 Epiphany*

GIVE THANKS for the Church of the Province of Central Africa.

Monday—24: *St. Matthias.*
Botswana; Central Zambia. *(Central Africa)*

Tuesday—25: Central Zimbabwe (The Lundi), **Eastern Zambia.** *(Central Africa)*

Wednesday—26: Harare; Lake Malawi. *(Central Africa)*

Thursday—27: Lusaka; Manicaland. *(Central Africa)*

Friday—28: Matabeleland; Northern Zambia. *(Central Africa)*

Saturday—March 1: Northern Malawi; Southern Malawi. *(Central Africa)*

WEEK OF MARCH 2, 2003 *Last Epiphany*

GIVE THANKS for the Anglican Church in Mexico.

Monday—3: Cuernavaca. *(Mexico)*

Tuesday—4: *Shrove Tuesday.*

Mexico. *(Mexico)*

Wednesday—5: *Ash Wednesday.*

ACCEPT our repentance, Lord, for the wrongs we have done: for our blindness to human need and suffering, and our indifference to injustice and cruelty.

Thursday—6: Northern Mexico. *(Mexico)*

Friday—7: Southeastern Mexico. *(Mexico)*

Saturday—8: Western Mexico. *(Mexico)*

WEEK OF MARCH 9, 2003 *Lent 1*

GIVE THANKS for the Province of Episcopal Church of Rwanda (PEER) (Eglise Episcopale au Rwanda) (Provinsi y'Itorero ry'Ubwepikopi mu Rwanda).

Monday—10: Butare; Byumba. (*Rwanda*)

Tuesday—11: Cyangugu; Gahini. (*Rwanda)*

Wednesday—12: Kibungo. (*Rwanda*)

Thursday—13: Kigali. (*Rwanda*)

Friday—14: Kigeme. (*Rwanda)*

Saturday—15: Shyira; Shyogwe. (*Rwanda*)

WEEK OF MARCH 16, 2003 *Lent 2*

GIVE THANKS for the Church of Ireland.

Monday—17: *St. Patrick.*

PRAY for peace in Northern Ireland.

Dublin and Glendalough; Limerick and Killaloe; Meath and Kildare. (Dublin, *Ireland*)

Tuesday—18: Cashel and Ossory; Cork, Cloyne and Ross. (Dublin, *Ireland*)

Wednesday—19: *St. Joseph.*

Armagh; Clogher; Connor. (Armagh, *Ireland*)

Thursday—20: Derry and Raphoe; Down and Dromore. (Armagh, *Ireland*)

Friday—21: Kilmore, Elphin and Ardagh. (Armagh, *Ireland*)

Saturday—22: Tuam, Killala and Achonry. (Armagh, *Ireland*)

WEEK OF MARCH 23, 2003 *Lent 3*

GIVE THANKS for the Church of England.

Monday—24: Bath and Wells; Birmingham; Bristol; Canterbury; Chelmsford. (Canterbury, *England*)

Tuesday—25: *The Annunciation of Our Lord Jesus Christ to the Blessed Virgin Mary.*

PRAY for the Mothers' Union.

Chichester; Coventry; Derby; Ely; Europe. (Canterbury, *England*)

Wednesday—26: Exeter; Gloucester; Guildford; Hereford; Leicester. (Canterbury, *England*)

Thursday—27: Lichfield; Lincoln; London; Norwich; Oxford. (Canterbury, *England*)

Friday—28: Peterborough; Portsmouth; Rochester; St. Albans; St. Edmundsbury and Ipswich. (Canterbury, *England*)

Saturday—29: Salisbury; Southwark; Truro; Winchester; Worcester. (Canterbury, *England*)

WEEK OF MARCH 30, 2003 *Lent 4*
Mothering Sunday

GIVE THANKS for the Church of South India.

Monday—31: Chennai; Coimbatore; Dornakal; East Kerala. *(South India)*

Tuesday—April 1: Jaffna (Sri Lanka); **Kanyakumari; Karimnagar.** *(South India)*

Wednesday—2: Karnataka Central; Karnataka North; Karnataka South. *(South India)*

Thursday—3: Krishna-Godavari; Madhya Kerala; Madurai-Ramnad; Medak. *(South India)*

Friday—4: Nandyal; North Kerala; Rayalaseema; South Kerala. *(South India)*

Saturday—5: Tirunelveli; Trichy-Tanjore; Vellore. *(South India)*

WEEK OF APRIL 6, 2003 *Lent 5*
(Passion Sunday)

GIVE THANKS for the Episcopal Church of the Sudan.

PRAY for the persecuted church.

Monday—7: Bor; Cueibet; El-Obeid; Ezzo. *(The Sudan)*

Tuesday—8: Ibba; Juba; Kadugli and Nuba Mountains; Kajokeji. *(The Sudan)*

Wednesday—9: Khartoum; Lainya; Lui; Malakal. *(The Sudan)*

Thursday—10: Maridi; Mundri; Port Sudan; Rejaf. *(The Sudan)*

Friday—11: Renk; Rokon; Rumbeck; Torit. *(The Sudan)*

Saturday—12: Wau; Yambio; Yei; Yirol. *(The Sudan)*

WEEK OF APRIL 13, 2003 *Palm Sunday*

ALMIGHTY AND EVERLIVING GOD, in your tender love for the human family you sent your Son our Savior Jesus Christ to take upon him our nature, and to suffer death upon the cross, giving us the example of his great humility: Mercifully grant that we may walk in the way of his suffering, and also share in his resurrection.

GIVE THANKS for the Church in Jerusalem and the Middle East.

Monday in Holy Week—14: Cyprus and the Gulf. *(Jerusalem and the Middle East)*

Tuesday in Holy Week—15: Egypt. *(Jerusalem and the Middle East)*

Wednesday in Holy Week—16: Iran. *(Jerusalem and the Middle East)*

Thursday—17: *Maundy Thursday.*

ALMIGHTY FATHER, whose dear Son, on the night before he suffered, instituted the Sacrament of his Body and Blood: Mercifully grant that we may receive it thankfully in remembrance of Jesus Christ our Lord.

Friday—18: *Good Friday.*

PRAY for peace in the Holy Land.

Jerusalem. (*Jerusalem and the Middle East*)

Holy Saturday—19: LORD, help us understand the silence of your tomb.

WEEK OF APRIL 20, 2003 *Easter Day*

REJOICE NOW, heavenly hosts and choirs of angels, and let your trumpets shout Salvation for the victory of our mighty King.

Rejoice and sing now, all the round earth, bright with a glorious splendor, for darkness has been vanquished by our eternal King.

Rejoice and be glad now, Mother Church, and let your holy courts, in radiant light, resound with the praises of your people.

Monday in Easter Week—21: REJOICE for God's promise of eternal life.

Tuesday in Easter Week—22: GIVE THANKS for the Communion of Saints.

Wednesday in Easter Week—23: PRAISE GOD that, in and through the Sacrament of Baptism, we have been received as His sons and daughters.

Thursday in Easter Week—24: PRAY we may be ever-faithful witnesses of Christ's death and resurrection.

Friday in Easter Week—25: PRAY we may walk in love, as Christ loved us.

Saturday in Easter Week—26: PROCLAIM: Alleluia! Alleluia! Christ is risen!

WEEK OF APRIL 27, 2003 *Easter 2*

GIVE THANKS for The Scottish Episcopal Church.

Monday—28: *St. Mark* (Trans).
Aberdeen and Orkney. *(Scotland)*

Tuesday—29: Argyll and the Isles. *(Scotland)*

Wednesday—30: Brechin; Edinburgh. *(Scotland)*

Thursday—May 1: *Saints Philip and James.*
Glasgow and Galloway. *(Scotland)*

Friday—2: Moray, Ross, and Caithness. *(Scotland)*

Saturday—3: St. Andrews, Dunkeld and Dunblane. *(Scotland)*

WEEK OF MAY 4, 2003 *Easter 3*

Theological Education Sunday

PRAY for seminaries and schools of theology that train clergy and laity in the Christian faith.

Monday—5: PRAY for Christian Education in parish churches.

Tuesday—6: PRAY for Anglican schools.

Wednesday—7: GIVE THANKS for Sunday School teachers and catechists.

Thursday—8: PRAY for Deans, faculty, instructors and students of Anglican seminaries.

Friday—9: PRAY for those seeking Holy Orders.

Saturday—10: PRAY for all who seek a deeper knowledge of Christ and of the faith.

WEEK OF MAY 11, 2003 *Easter 4*

GIVE THANKS for the Anglican Church of Korea.

Monday—12: Pusan. *(Korea)*

Tuesday—13: Seoul. *(Korea)*

Wednesday—14: Taejon. *(Korea)*

Thursday—15: PRAY for all in Religious Orders.

Friday—16: PRAY for the work of the Anglican-Roman Catholic International Commission.

Saturday—17: PRAY for all bishops, priests and deacons.

WEEK OF MAY 18, 2003 *Easter 5*

GIVE THANKS for the Church of the Province of Uganda.

Monday—19: Bukedi; Bunyoro; Busoga; Central Buganda. *(Uganda)*

Tuesday—20: East Ankole; Kampala; Karamoja; Kigezi; Kinkizi. *(Uganda)*

Wednesday—21: Kitgum; Kumi; Lango; Luwero. *(Uganda)*

Thursday—22: Madi and West Nile; Mbale; Mityana; Muhabura; Mukono; Namirembe. *(Uganda)*

Friday—23: Nebbi; North Kigezi; North Mbale; Northern Uganda; Ruwenzori. *(Uganda)*

Saturday—24: Sebei; Soroti; South Rwenzori; West Ankole; West Buganda. *(Uganda)*

WEEK OF MAY 25, 2003 *Easter 6*

Anglican Communion Sunday

PRAY for the Anglican Communion, the Anglican Consultative Council (ACC), for the Secretary General and the Anglican Communion Office staff.

Monday—26: *St. Augustine of Canterbury.*

PRAY for Archbishop of Canterbury Rowan Williams.

Tuesday—27: PRAY for the Anglican Communion: its witness to the Faith of Christ, its people and clergy.

Wednesday—28: PRAY for the Anglican Consultative Council.

Thursday—29: *Ascension Day.*

GIVE THANKS for the Anglican Observer to the United Nations and staff.

Friday—30: PRAY for the Anglican Communion Secretary General and the Anglican Communion Office Staff.

Saturday—31: *The Visitation of the Blessed Virgin Mary.* PRAY for the courage to carry Christ within us and present him wherever we go.

WEEK OF JUNE 1, 2003 *Easter 7*
Ascension Sunday

Anglican Communications Sunday

PRAY for the communication of the Gospel to all the World.

Monday—2: PRAY for religious communicators: writers, editors, observers; authors and poets; for religious artists and musicians; and for all those who seek to spread the Gospel and the faith of Jesus Christ to every person, in every part of the world.

Tuesday—3: PRAY for the ministry of the written Word.

Wednesday—4: PRAY for the ministry of the spoken Word.

Thursday—5: PRAY for the ministry of those who translate the Word into other languages, in braille or by voice recording.

Friday—6: PRAY for the ministry of the healing Word, and for those whose gift of God's grace through touch restores the sick or broken-hearted

Saturday—7: PRAY for the ministry of the Word in truth and in love, that it may unite us.

WEEK OF JUNE 8, 2003 *Pentecost*
Whitsunday

PRAY for all church musicians: Organist-choirmasters, choristers, composers, musicians and small voices that give praise to God.

Monday—9: GIVE THANKS for Retreat Houses and church conference centers.

Tuesday—10: GIVE THANKS for the service of those who care for our church buildings and property.

Wednesday—11: *St. Barnabas.*

PRAY for those who care for the poor.

Thursday—12: PRAY for those who feed the hungry.

Friday—13: PRAY for those who shelter the homeless.

Saturday—14: PRAY for those who mourn.

WEEK OF JUNE 15, 2003 *Trinity Sunday*

GIVE THANKS for the Anglican Church of Papua New Guinea.

Monday—16: Aipo Rongo. *(Papua New Guinea)*

Tuesday—17: Dogura. *(Papua New Guinea)*

Wednesday—18: New Guinea Islands. *(Papua New Guinea)*

Thursday—19: *Corpus Christi.*

Port Moresby. *(Papua New Guinea)*

Friday—20: Popondota. *(Papua New Guinea)*

Saturday—21: REJOICE in all things bright and beautiful.

WEEK OF JUNE 22, 2003 *2 Pentecost*

Sundays may be after Pentecost, Trinity or Ordinary Time. Custom varies around the Communion.

GIVE THANKS for the Church in Pakistan.

Monday—23: Arabian Gulf; Faisalabad. *(Pakistan)*

Tuesday—24: *Nativity of St. John the Baptist.*
Hyderabad. *(Pakistan)*

Wednesday—25: Karachi. *(Pakistan)*

Thursday—26: Lahore. *(Pakistan)*

Friday—27: Multan; Peshawar. *(Pakistan)*

Saturday—28: Raiwind; Sialkot. *(Pakistan)*

WEEK OF JUNE 29, 2003 *3 Pentecost*

GIVE THANKS for the Anglican Church of the Central American Region (La Iglesia Anglicana de la Región Central de America [IARCA]).

Monday—30: *Saints Peter and Paul, Apostles* (Trans).
Costa Rica. *(Central America)*

Tuesday—July 1: El Salvador. *(Central America)*

Wednesday—2: Guatemala. *(Central America)*

Thursday—3: Nicaragua. *(Central America)*

Friday—4: GIVE THANKS and PRAY for those who stand watch to guard, protect and rescue us: fire brigades, police officers, ambulance and emergency medical personnel.

Saturday—5: Panama. *(Central America)*

WEEK OF JULY 6, 2003 *4 Pentecost*

GIVE THANKS for the Church of North India.

Monday—7: Agra; Amritsar; Andaman and Car Nicobar Islands; Barrackpore. *(North India)*

Tuesday—8: Bhopal; Calcutta; Chandigarh; Chotanagpur. *(North India)*

Wednesday—9: Cuttack; Delhi; Durgapur; Eastern Himalayas; Gujarat. *(North India)*

Thursday—10: Jabalpur; Kolhapur; Lucknow; Marathwada; Mumbai (formerly Bombay). *(North India)*

Friday—11: *St. Benedict.*

Nagpur; Nasik; North East India; Patna. *(North India)*

Saturday—12: Phulbani; Pune; Rajasthan; Sambalpur. *(North India)*

WEEK OF JULY 13, 2003 *5 Pentecost*

GIVE THANKS for the Church of Bangladesh.

Monday—14: Dhaka. *(Bangladesh)*

Tuesday—15: Kushtia. *(Bangladesh)*

Wednesday—16: GIVE thanks for the gift of friendship.

Thursday—17: PRAY for church hospitals: for their staffs and for those they serve.

Friday—18: PRAY for those in prisons, and those who minister to them.

Saturday—19: PRAY for refugees.

GIVE THANKS for the Church of Nigeria (Anglican Communion).

Monday—21: *Province I:* **Akoko; Akure; Benin; Egba; Ekiti; Ekiti West; Ibadan; Ibadan North; Ibadan South; Ife; Igbomina.** *(Nigeria)*

Tuesday—22: *St. Mary Magdalene.*

Province I: **Ijebu; Ikale-Ilaje; Ilesa; Kabba; Kwara; Lagos; Lagos West; Lokoja; Offa; Oke-Osun; Ondo; Osun; Owo; Remo; Sabongidda-Ora; Ughelli; Warri; Yewa (Egbado).** *(Nigeria)*

Wednesday—23: *Province II:* **Aba; Abakaliki; Asaba; Awka; Calabar; Egbu; Enugu; Esan; Ideato; Ikka; Mbaise; The Niger Delta; Niger Delta North; Niger Delta West.** *(Nigeria)*

Thursday—24: *Province II:* **Nnewi; Nsukka; Oji River; Okigwe North; Okigwe South; Oleh; On the Niger; Orlu; Owerri; Ukwa; Umuahia; Uyo.** *(Nigeria)*

Friday—25: *St. James the Apostle.*

Province III: **Abuja; Bauchi; Bida; Damaturu; Dutse; Gombe; Gusau; Gwagwalada; Jalingo; Jos; Kaduna; Kafanchan.** *(Nigeria)*

Saturday—26: *Province III:* **Kano; Katsina; Kebbi; Lafia; Maiduguri; Makurdi; Minna; Oturkpo; Sokoto; Wusasa; Yola.** *(Nigeria)*

WEEK OF JULY 27, 2003 *7 Pentecost*

GIVE THANKS for the Church of the Southern Cone (Iglesia Anglicana del Cono Sur de America).

Monday—28: Argentina; Northern Argentina. *(Southern Cone)*

Tuesday—29: Bolivia. *(Southern Cone)*

Wednesday—30: Chile. *(Southern Cone)*

Thursday—31: Paraguay. *(Southern Cone)*

Friday—August 1: Peru. *(Southern Cone)*

Saturday—2: Uruguay. *(Southern Cone)*

WEEK OF AUGUST 3, 2003 *8 Pentecost*

GIVE THANKS for the extra-provincial Episcopal Church of Cuba (Iglesia Episcopal de Cuba).

Monday—4: PRAY for the Chapel Royal, and for all chapels.

Tuesday—5: PRAY for religious peculiars: chapels in hospitals or airports, on military bases or scientific research stations.

Wednesday—6: *Transfiguration of Our Lord.*

GIVE THANKS for those who serve in Hospice ministry to the dying.

Thursday—7: GIVE THANKS for Sacristans and those who serve on Altar Guilds.

Friday—8: THANK GOD for the work and ministry of Anglican Religious.

Saturday—9: PRAISE GOD for the gift of love and for the capacity to love.

WEEK OF AUGUST 10, 2003 *9 Pentecost*

GIVE THANKS for the Province of Melanesia.

Monday—11: Banks and Torres; Vanuatu, Vanuatu. *(Melanesia)*

Tuesday—12: Central Melanesia, Melanesia. *(Melanesia)*

Wednesday—13: Central Solomons; Hanuato'o, Solomon Islands. *(Melanesia)*

Thursday—14: Malaita, Solomon Islands. *(Melanesia)*

Friday—15: *St. Mary the Virgin (Assumption/ Dormition).*

Temotu, Solomon Islands. *(Melanesia)*

Saturday—16: Ysabel, Solomon Islands. *(Melanesia)*

WEEK OF AUGUST 17, 2003 *10 Pentecost*

THANK GOD for the generosity of those who give abundantly of their time, talent and treasure for the spread of the Kingdom of God.

Monday—18: PRAY for the ministry of Acolytes.

Tuesday—19: PRAY for the ministry of Lectors.

Wednesday—20: PRAY for Abbeys, monasteries and convents.

Thursday—21: PRAY for Anglican Pilgrimage Centres: Walsingham, Holy Island, Haddington, Ugandan Martyrs, Bernard Mizeki Center, Glastonbury, Llanthony, Chichester, Canterbury, St. Albans, Winchester, Jerusalem, Durham, and all others.

Friday—22: PRAY for families.

Saturday—23: GIVE THANKS for the Mar Thoma Syrian Church.

WEEK OF AUGUST 24, 2003 *11 Pentecost*

GIVE THANKS for the Church of the Province of West Africa.

Monday—25: *St. Bartholomew* (Trans).
Cameroon (Region Missionaire). *(West Africa)*

Tuesday—26: Accra; Cape Coast; Koforidua; Kumasi; Sekondi; Sunyani; Tamale, Ghana. *(West Africa)*

Wednesday—27: Guinea. *(West Africa)*

Thursday—28: Liberia. *(West Africa)*

Friday—29: Bo; Freetown, Sierra Leone. *(West Africa)*

Saturday—30: Gambia, The Gambia. *(West Africa)*

WEEK OF AUGUST 31, 2003 *12 Pentecost*

GIVE THANKS for the Anglican Church in Aotearoa, New Zealand and Polynesia.

Monday—September 1: Aotearoa (South Island; Southern Region; Northern Region; East Coast Region). *(Aotearoa, New Zealand and Polynesia)*

Tuesday—2: Auckland; Christchurch; New Zealand. *(Aotearoa, New Zealand and Polynesia)*

Wednesday—3: Dunedin; Nelson; New Zealand. *(Aotearoa, New Zealand and Polynesia)*

Thursday—4: Polynesia. *(Aotearoa, New Zealand and Polynesia)*

Friday—5: Waiapu, New Zealand. *(Aotearoa, New Zealand and Polynesia)*

Saturday—6: Waikato; Wellington; New Zealand. *(Aotearoa, New Zealand and Polynesia)*

WEEK OF SEPTEMBER 7, 2003 *13 Pentecost*

GIVE THANKS for the Episcopal Church of the United States of America.

Monday—8: *Nativity of the Blessed Virgin Mary.*

Province V: **Chicago; Eastern Michigan; Eau Claire; Fond du Lac; Indianapolis; Michigan; Milwaukee; Missouri; Northern Indiana; Northern Michigan; Ohio; Quincy; Southern Ohio; Springfield; Western Michigan.**

Tuesday—9: *Province VIII*: **Alaska; Arizona; California; Eastern Oregon; El Camino Real; Hawaii; Idaho; Los Angeles; Navajoland Area Mission; Nevada; Northern California; Olympia; Oregon; San Diego; San Joaquin; Spokane; Utah; Taiwan.**

Wednesday—10: *Province IV*: **Alabama; Atlanta; Central Florida; Central Gulf Coast; East Carolina; East Tennessee; Florida; Georgia; Kentucky; Lexington; Louisiana; Mississippi; North Carolina; South Carolina; Southeast Florida; Southwest Florida; Tennessee; Upper South Carolina; West Tennessee; Western North Carolina.**

Thursday—11: *Province II*: **New York; Newark; Albany; Central New York; Convocation of American Churches in Europe; Haiti; Long Island; New Jersey; Rochester; Virgin Islands; Western New York; Micronesia.**

Friday—12: *Province III*: **West Virginia; Bethlehem; Central Pennsylvania; Delaware; Easton; Maryland; Northwestern Pennsylvania; Pennsylvania; Southwestern Virginia; Virginia; Washington; Southern Virginia; Pittsburgh.**

Saturday—13: *Province VII*: **Arkansas; Dallas; Fort Worth; Kansas; Northwest Texas; Oklahoma; Rio Grande; Texas; West Missouri; West Texas; Western Kansas; Western Louisiana.**

WEEK OF SEPTEMBER 14, 2003 *14 Pentecost*

We continue praying for The Episcopal Church, the United States of America.

Monday—15: *Holy Cross Day* (Trans).

Province VI: **Colorado; Iowa; Minnesota; Montana; Nebraska; North Dakota; South Dakota; Wyoming.**

Tuesday—16: *Province IX*: **Central Ecuador; Columbia; Dominican Republic; Honduras; Litoral (Ecuador).**

Wednesday—17: *Province I:* **Connecticut; Maine; Massachusetts; New Hampshire; Rhode Island; Vermont; Western Massachusetts.**

Thursday—18: PRAY for the Bishop Suffragan for the Armed Services, Healthcare and Prison Ministries; PRAY for Military, Hospital and Prison Chaplains. *(United States of America)*

Friday—19: PRAY for The Bishop Ordinary to the Canadian Forces, and Chaplains serving in the Chaplain Branch. *(Canada)*

Saturday—20: PRAY for First Nation people and clergy of Canada. *(Canada)*

WEEK OF SEPTEMBER 21, 2003 *15 Pentecost*

GIVE THANKS for the Anglican Church of Canada (L'Eglise Anglicane du Canada).

Monday—22: *St. Matthew* (Trans).

British Columbia; Caledonia; Anglican Parishes of the Central Interior (formerly Cariboo); Kootenay; New Westminster; Yukon. (British Columbia and the Yukon, *Canada)*

Tuesday—23: Central Newfoundland; Eastern Newfoundland and Labrador; Fredericton; Montreal; Canada. (Canada, *Canada*)

Wednesday—24: Nova Scotia and Prince Edward Island; Quebec; Western Newfoundland; Canada. (Canada, *Canada*)

Thursday—25: The Arctic; Athabasca; Brandon; Calgary; Edmonton; Canada. (Rupert's Land, *Canada*)

Friday—26: Keewatin; Qu'Appelle; Rupert's Land; Saskatchewan; Saskatoon; Canada. (Rupert's Land, *Canada*)

Saturday—27: Algoma; Huron; Moosonee; Niagara; Ontario; Ottawa; Toronto. (Ontario, *Canada*)

WEEK OF SEPTEMBER 28, 2003 *16 Pentecost*

GIVE THANKS for the Church of Nippon Sei Ko Kai (The Anglican Communion in Japan).

Monday—29: *St. Michael and All Angels—Michaelmas.*

Chubu; Hokkaido. *(Japan)*

Tuesday—30: Kita Kanto; Kobe. *(Japan)*

Wednesday—October 1: Kyoto; Kyushu. *(Japan)*

Thursday—2: Okinawa; Osaka. *(Japan)*

Friday—3: Tohoku; Tokyo. *(Japan)*

Saturday—4: *St. Francis.*

Yokohama. *(Japan)*

WEEK OF OCTOBER 5, 2003 *17 Pentecost*

GIVE THANKS for the Church in the Province of the West Indies.

Monday—6: Jamaica (Cayman Islands; Montego Bay; Mandeville). (*West Indies*)

Tuesday—7: Nassau and the Bahamas, Bahamas. (*West Indies*)

Wednesday—8: North Eastern Caribbean and Aruba. (*West Indies*)

Thursday—9: Trinidad and Tobago; Barbados. (*West Indies*)

Friday—10: Windward Islands. (*West Indies*)

Saturday—11: Belize; Guyana. (*West Indies*)

WEEK OF OCTOBER 12, 2003 *18 Pentecost*

GIVE THANKS for the province of York in the Church of England.

Monday—13: Blackburn; Bradford. (York, *England)*

Tuesday—14: Carlisle; Chester; Durham. (York, *England)*

Wednesday—15: Liverpool; Manchester. (York, *England)*

Thursday—16: Newcastle; Ripon and Leeds; Sheffield. (York, *England)*

Friday—17: Sodor and Man; Southwell. (York, *England)*

Saturday—18: *St. Luk*e.

Wakefield; York. (York, *England)*

WEEK OF OCTOBER 19, 2003 *19 Pentecost*

GIVE THANKS for the Anglican Church of Tanzania.

Monday—20: Central Tanganyika; Dar-es Salaam; Kagera; Kondoa. *(Tanzania)*

Tuesday—21: Mara; Masasi; Morogoro. *(Tanzania)*

Wednesday—22: Mount Kilimanjaro; Mpwapwa; Rift Valley. *(Tanzania)*

Thursday—23: *St. James of Jerusalem.*

Ruaha; Ruvuma; South West Tanganyika. *(Tanzania)*

Friday—24: Southern Highlands; Tabora; Tanga; Victoria Nyanza. *(Tanzania)*

Saturday—25: Western Tanganyika; Zanzibar. *(Tanzania)*

WEEK OF OCTOBER 26, 2003 *20 Pentecost*

GIVE THANKS for the Church of South East Asia.

Monday—27: Kuching, Malaysia. *(South East Asia)*

Tuesday—28: *Saints Simon and Jude.*

Sabah, Malaysia. *(South East Asia)*

Wednesday—29: Singapore, Singapore. *(South East Asia)*

Thursday—30: West Malaysia, Malaysia. *(South East Asia)*

Friday—31: *All Hallows Eve.*

GIVE THANKS for the Old Catholic churches.

Saturday—November 1: *All Saints' Day.*

PRAY for all the Saints who have illumined the world with their faith and witness to Jesus Christ.

WEEK OF NOVEMBER 2, 2003 *21 Pentecost/ All Saints' Sunday*

GIVE THANKS for the Church in Wales.

Monday—3: *All Souls* (Trans).

St. Asaph. *(Wales)*

Tuesday—4: Bangor. *(Wales)*

Wednesday—5: St. David's. *(Wales)*

Thursday—6: Llandaff. *(Wales)*

Friday—7: Swansea and Brecon. *(Wales)*

Saturday—8: Monmouth. *(Wales)*

WEEK OF NOVEMBER 9, 2003 *22 Pentecost*

GIVE THANKS for the Province of the Anglican Church of Congo (Province de L'Eglise Anglicane du Congo).

Monday—10: Boga. *(Congo)*

Tuesday—11: Bukavu. *(Congo)*

Wednesday—12: Kisangani. *(Congo)*

Thursday—13: Katanga. *(Congo)*

Friday—14: Nord-Kivu. *(Congo)*

Saturday—15: Kindu. *(Congo)*

WEEK OF NOVEMBER 16, 2003 *23 Pentecost*

GIVE THANKS for the extra-provincial Diocese of Puerto Rico.

Monday—17: GIVE THANKS for the extra-provincial Diocese of Venezuela.

Tuesday—18: GIVE THANKS for the extra-provincial Diocese of the Falkland Islands.

Wednesday—19: GIVE THANKS for the extra-provincial Lusitanian Church of Portugal.

Thursday—20: GIVE THANKS for the Spanish Reformed Episcopal Church.

Friday—21: PRAY for children that they may grow to know and love God.

Saturday—22: *St. Cecelia.*

PRAY for young people that, having the confidence of their faith in Almighty God, they may resist the temptations of the world.

WEEK OF NOVEMBER 23, 2003 *Last Pentecost: Christ the King*

GIVE THANKS for the Episcopal Anglican Church of Brazil (Igreaja Episcopal Anglicana Do Brasil).

Monday—24: São Paulo, Brazil. (*Brazil*)

Tuesday—25: Southern Brazil, Brazil. (*Brazil*)

Wednesday—26: Southwestern Brazil, Brazil. (*Brazil*)

Thursday—27: Rio de Janeiro, Brazil. (*Brazil*)

Friday—28: Recife, Brazil. *(Brazil)*

Saturday—29: Brasilia; Pelotas; Brazil. *(Brazil)*

WEEK OF November 30, 2003 *Advent 1*

GIVE THANKS for the Anglican Church of Kenya.

Monday—December 1: *St. Andrew* (Trans).

Bondo; Bungoma; Butere; Eldoret; Embu. *(Kenya)*

Tuesday—2: Kajiado; Katakwa; Kirinyaga; Kitale; Kitui. *(Kenya)*

Wednesday—3: Machakos; Maseno North; Maseno South; Maseno West. *(Kenya)*

Thursday—4: Mbeere; Meru; Mombasa; Mount Kenya Central; Mount Kenya South. *(Kenya)*

Friday—5: Mount Kenya West; Nairobi; Nakuru; Nambale. *(Kenya)*

Saturday—6: *St. Nicholas.*

Nyahururu; Taita-Taveta; Thika. *(Kenya)*

WEEK OF DECEMBER 7, 2003 *Advent 2*

GIVE THANKS for the Episcopal Church in the Philippines (Iglesia Episkopal sa Philipinas).

Monday—8: *Conception of Mary.*

Central Philippines. *(The Philippines)*

Tuesday—9: North Central Philippines. *(The Philippines)*

Wednesday—10: Northern Luzon. *(The Philippines)*

Thursday—11: Northern Philippines. *(The Philippines)*

Friday—12: *Nuestra Señora de Guadalupe (Americas).*

Southern Philippines. *(The Philippines)*

Saturday—13: *St. Lucy.*

Santiago. *(The Philippines)*

PRAY for evangelism: for the increase of the family of Christian faith; that we may each be a willing and bold ambassador of God.

WEEK OF DECEMBER 14, 2003 *Advent 3*

GIVE THANKS for the Church of the Province of Southern Africa.

Monday—15: Angola; Bloemfontein; Cape Town; Christ the King. *(Southern Africa)*

Tuesday—16: George; Grahamstown; Highveld; Johannesburg. *(Southern Africa)*

Wednesday—17: Kimberley and Kuruman; Klerksdorp; Lebombo; Lesotho. *(Southern Africa)*

Thursday—18: Namibia; Natal; Niassa; Port Elizabeth. *(Southern Africa)*

Friday—19: Pretoria; St. Helena; St. John's; St. Mark the Evangelist. *(Southern Africa)*

Saturday—20: Swaziland; Umzimvubu; Zululand. *(Southern Africa)*

PRAY for the Church of God throughout the world.

Monday—22: *St. Thomas* (Trans).

PRAY for those who seek Christ and a deeper knowledge of him.

Tuesday—23: PRAY for those who believe themselves hopeless; that they may find hope in Him who gives hope and peace to hearts.

Wednesday—24: *Christmas Eve.*

PRAY that our hearts may always be open to the joy and wonder of God's mighty works.

Thursday—25:

The Nativity of Our Lord—Christmas Day.

O GOD, you make us glad by the yearly festival of the birth of your only son Jesus Christ: Grant that we, who joyfully receive him as our Redeemer, may with sure confidence behold him when he comes to be our Judge; who lives and reigns with you and the Holy Spirit, one God, now and for ever. Amen.

Friday—26: *St. Stephen.*

PRAY for all who suffer, are persecuted or threatened for the Christian faith.

Saturday—27: *St. John the Evangelist.*

PRAY for missionaries.

GIVE THANKS for the Church of Ceylon.

Monday—29: *Holy Innocents* (Trans).

PRAY for children everywhere, that they may never face danger anywhere.

Tuesday—30: *St. Thomas á Becket* (Trans).

Colombo, Sri Lanka. (*Ceylon*)

Wednesday—31: *New Year's Eve.*

Kurunagala, Sri Lanka. (*Ceylon*).

PRAY for the blessings of peace in the New Year to come.

English Lord's Prayer
Our Father

Our Father, who art in heaven,
hallowed be thy Name,
thy kingdom come,
thy will be done,
on earth as it is in heaven.
Give us this day our daily bread.
And forgive us our trespasses,
as we forgive those
who tresspass against us.
And lead us not into temptation,
but deliver us from evil.
For thine is the kingdom,
and the power, and the glory,
forever and ever. Amen.

Spanish Lord's Prayer
Padrenuestro

Padre nuestro que estás en el cielo,
santificado sea tu Nombre
venga tu reino,
hágase to voluntad,
en la tierra como en el cielo.
Danos hoy nuestro pan de cada día.
perdona nuestras ofensas,
como también nosotros perdonamos
a los que nos ofenden.
No nos dejes caer en tentación
y líbranos del mal.
Porque tuyo es el reino,
tuyo es el poder,
y tuya es el poder,
y tuya es la gloria,
ahora y por siempre.
Amén.

French Lord's Prayer
Notre Père

Notre Père, qui es aux cieux,
que ton Nom soit sanctifié,
que ton règne vienne.
Que ta volonté soit faite
sur la terre comme au ciel.
Donne-nous aujourd'hui notre pain de ce jour.
Pardonne-nous nos offenses,
comme nous pardonnons aussi
à ceux qui nous ont offensés.
Et ne nous soumets pas à la tentation,
mais délivre-nous du mal.
Car c'est à toi qu'appartiennent le règne,
la puissance et la gloire,
dans les siècles, Amen.

Portuguese Lord's Prayer
Pai Nosso

Pai nosso que estás no céu,
Santificado seja o Teu Nome.
Venha o Teu Reino.
Seja feita a tua vontade,
Assim no terra como no céu.
O pão nosso de cada dia nos dá hoje.
Perdoa-nos as nossas dívidas
Assim como nós também perdoamos
aos nossos devedores.
E não nos deixes cair
em tentação, mas livra-nos do mal,
Pois Teu é o Reino, o Poder
e a Glória para sempre.
Amém

Swahili Lord's Prayer
Sala ya Bwana

Baba yetu
uliye mbinguni,
Jina lako litukuzwe,
Ufalme wako uje,
Mapenzi yako yatimizwe
hapa duniani kama huko mbinguni.
Utupe leo riziki yetu,
Utusamehe makosa yetu
Kama sisi tunavyowasamehe waliotukosa.
Usitutie majaribuni
lakini utuokoe na yule Mwovu,
Kwa kuwa ufalme ni wako,
na nguvu, na utukufu
hata milele.
Amina.

Japanese Lord's Prayer
主の祈り

天にいますわたしたちの父よ、
み名が聖とされますように。
み国が来ますように。
み心が天に行われるとおり、
地にも行われますように。
日ごとの食物を今日も与えてください。
わたしたちに対して罪のある者を
赦していますから、
わたしたちの罪も赦してください。
わたしたちを試みに陥らせずに、
悪から救い出してください。
み国も力も栄光も、
世々に限りなく主のものだからです。
アーメン

The Anglican Communion exists on every continent, and is a fellowship—within the One, Holy, Catholic, and Apostolic Church—of churches in communion with one another and with the See of Canterbury. The relationship is based on a common history deriving from the Church of England, a common tradition of doctrine, discipline and worship, and mutual responsibility and interdependence in their mission. It is a freely chosen partnership with emphasis on autonomy and independence. The Archbishop of Canterbury, honored as "first among equals," is a symbol of unity and frequently serves as our spokesman in international and ecumenical affairs. Other symbols of unity are The Book of Common Prayer—in many different versions and translations—and the Lambeth Conference, which brings together all diocesan bishops for consultations once a decade. English language and culture, formerly important bonds of unity, are now less significant as the Communion grows rapidly in Africa, Asia and in other non-English-speaking regions.

A Diocese is a geographical aggregation of parishes and mission congregations under the administrative and pastoral care of a bishop. In Anglican tradition a "local church" consists of all who share the leadership of the same bishop. A goal of Anglican mission is to establish an independent church in each country where Anglicans are found in sufficient numbers to make this possible.

Provinces: There are many provinces in the Anglican Communion, each one indicating a national church or geographical area incorporating a number of dioceses. They are usually under the leadership of an Archbishop or a Presiding Bishop who serves as the primate. There are two kinds of provinces: one, an autonomous church in the Anglican

Communion, as the Province of Melanesia; and two, a regional cluster of dioceses within a large national church, an internal or ecclesiastical province, as found in England, Canada or the United States.

Lambeth: As the Anglican Church spread during the 19th century, it was felt desirable that all diocesan bishops should meet together from time to time, to coordinate planning, strengthen the bonds of unity, and to consult about major issues. The first Lambeth Conference was in 1867 at Lambeth Palace, the residence of the Archbishop of Canterbury. Conferences are held about every ten years. 1998 was a Conference year.

The Anglican Consultative Council (ACC), with a permanent staff headed by a Secretary General, meets once every two or three years and consists of one, two or three members selected by each member Province. It includes bishops, priests and lay men and women who know what the church has to deal with in their own part of the world. The Archbishop of Canterbury is the president of the council and is chairman of the first session of each meeting.

The Primates Meeting: The Primates, or episcopal heads of the member churches of the Anglican Communion, meet regularly. The Primates assist in developing the agenda for meetings of the Anglican Consultative Council and the Lambeth Conference and plan for the implementation of their recommendations.

Inter-Anglican Networks: Composed of provincial specialists in a number of fields, these networks have been sponsored and assisted (but not funded) by the ACC. They include networks on Youth, Family, Ecumenical Relations, Liturgy, Peace and Justice issues, the Anglican Publishers Consortium, and the Mission Commission (MISSIO).

National Days of Anglican Communion Nations

Algeria	July 5, Independence Day
Antigua	November 1, National Day
Argentina	July 9, Independence Day
Australia	January 26, Australia Day
Bahamas	July 10, Independence Day
Bangladesh	March 26, Independence Day
Barbados	November 30, Independence Day
Belize	September 21, Independence Day
Bermuda	May 25, Bermuda Day
Bolivia	August 6, Independence Day
Botswana	Sept. 30-Oct. 1, Botswana Day
Brazil	September 7, Independence Day
Burundi	July 1, Independence Day
Canada	July 1, Canada Day
Chile	September 18, Independence Day
Colombia	July 20, Independence Day
Costa Rica	September 15, Central American Independence Day
Cuba	January 1, Liberation Day
Cyprus	July 1, Independence Day
Dominican Republic	February 27, Independence Day
Ecuador	Aug. 10, Independence Day
Egypt	July 23, Anniversary of the Revolution
El Salvador	September 15, Independence Day
England	April 23, St. George's Day
Ethiopia	October 10, Fiji Day
France	July 14, Bastille Day
Gambia	February 18, Independence Day
Grenada	February 7, Independence Day
Guatemala	September 15, Independence Day
Guinea	September 24, Independence Day
Guyana	February 23, Republic Day
Haiti	January 1, Independence Day

Honduras .... September 15, Independence Day
Hong Kong .... Last Monday in August, Liberation Day
India .... January 26, Independence Day
Iran .... April 1, Islamic Republic Day
Ireland .... March 17, St. Patrick's Day
Israel .... May 14, Independence Day
Jamaica .... First Monday in August, Independence Day
Japan .... February 11, National Foundation Day
Jordan .... May 25, Independence Day
Kenya .... December 12, Independence Day
Korea .... August 15, Independence Day or October 3, National Foundation Day
Lebanon .... November 22, Independence Day
Lesotho .... October 5, Independence Day
Liberia .... January 7, Pioneers Day
Libya .... December 24, Independence Day
Madagascar .... June 27, Independence Day
Malawi .... July 6, Independence Day
Malaysia .... August 31, National Day
Mauritius .... March 21, Independence Day
Mexico .... September 16, Independence Day
Mozambique .... June 25, Independence Day
Myanmar .... January 4, Independence Day
Namibia .... August 26, Independence Day
Nevis .... September 19, Independence Day
New Zealand .... February 6, Waitangi or New Zealand Day
Nicaragua .... September 15, Independence Day
Nigeria .... October 1, National Day
Pakistan .... August 14, Independence Day
Papua New Guinea .... September 16, Independence Day
Paraguay .... May 15, Independence Day
Peru .... July 28, Independence Day

Philippines	June 12, Independence Day
Portugal	June 10, National Day
Puerto Rico	July 25, Constitution Day
Rwanda	July 1, Independence Day
St. Kitts	September 19, Independence Day
St. Lucia	February 21, Independence Day
St. Vincent	October 27, Thanksgiving and Independence Day
Scotland	January 1, New Year's Day ("Hogmanay")
Seychelles	June 29, Independence Day
Sierra Leone	April 27, Independence Day
Singapore	August 9, Singapore National Day
Solomon Islands	July 7, Independence Day
South Africa	May 31, Republic Day
Spain	October 12, National Day
Sri Lanka	February 4, Independence Day
Sudan	January 1, Independence Day
Swaziland	September 6, Independence Day
Syria	April 17, Independence Day
Taiwan	January 1, Foundation of Republic of China
Tanzania	December 9, Independence Day
Trinidad & Tobago	August 31, Independence Day
Tunisia	March 20, Independence Day
Uganda	October 9, Independence Day
United States	July 4, Independence Day
Uruguay	August 25, Independence Day
Vanuatu	July 30, Independence Day
Venezuela	July 5, Independence Day
Wales	March 1, St. David's Day
Zaire	June 30, Independence Day
Zambia	October 24, Independence Day
Zimbabwe	April 19, Independence Day

Index